For my parents Rodwell
(1944–2023) and Juliet Dube

A SHORT

The stories that make our gardens

HISTORY

Illustrations by Sarah Jane Humphrey

OF

Advolly Richmond

FLOWERS

FRANCES
LINCOLN

CONTENTS

INTRODUCTION

As a garden and plant historian, I find that exploring the backgrounds of plants helps me to understand the changes that have occurred over the years since their introduction into cultivation. Regardless of how they arrived in Britain, the true origin and story of each of the flowers in this book go a long way back to other countries, even continents. Their stories are filled with tales of adventure, intrigue, piracy and, even, obsession and duplicity. The diversity in our garden flowers is a celebration of the endeavours and, in some cases, sacrifices of the people who located and recorded them.

Plants that are necessary for pharmacological and culinary use have been cultivated around the world for millennia. Equally, superior ornamental flowers were selected for use in cultural ceremonies, for example, the African marigold in the rituals of the Mexican Day of the Dead (see pages 174–175). As empires waxed and waned, plants were gathered and transported back to various countries and the spoils shared among the conquerors and colonisers alike.

Many flowers introduced to the West had been in cultivation in the Far and Middle East for hundreds of years and, like the tulip, arrived as beautiful formed objects of desire, which had been selected and improved from the local wild flora. The route, timing and point of introduction are not always known or indeed clear cut at all.

Between the sixteenth and nineteenth centuries, there was a huge influx of plants into Europe from around the world. While dedicated plant collectors and naturalists sought to furnish their mother country with as many new plants as possible, especially if they proved to be economically useful, many government employees serving overseas such as diplomats, trade officials and even their wives and children – also actively participated in the collection and introduction of the flowers that we find in our parks and gardens today.

But what became of the native names of these plants, scooped up in abundance and transported halfway round the world? Seemingly, they lost their identity the further they travelled from their homelands. They were transplanted into overly warm glasshouses or the cold, alien soil in which some perished. They received new names commemorating the very people who had plucked them from their familiar habitat, or revered fellow scientists or the rulers of their new found home. Queen Victoria being one such sovereign.

To the bewilderment of many gardeners, these names changed frequently and still do, therefore you will find plenty of historical nomenclature mischief in this book. This is not to irritate the gardener – at least I don't think so – but merely a necessary botanical process which we must endure as scientists discover more and more about the plants. Yes, I *am* looking at you, *Dicentra spectabilis* (see pages 102–3).

The idea behind this book is to demonstrate how seemingly ordinary garden plants, many of which I grow in my own garden, have a story embedded in their origins. I have not included in-depth botanical descriptions nor dwelt too long on the derivations of their names unless pertinent to the story I've recounted. Much of that information is readily available. In choosing the plants in this volume, I have tried to ensure that they are commercially available to you today, whether through everyday outlets or specialist nurseries.

The flowers will be familiar, many of them old garden favourites, some of which we first encountered in our childhoods, possibly at our parents', grandparents' or even great-grandparents' houses. Others may be associated with memories of holidays or honeymoons and form lasting impressions – each time we encounter their unique characteristics or a whiff of their scent, it immediately transports us back to these precious moments. Someone once said that a garden should be full of old faces, sights and scents.

Flowers have always featured very prominently in our society, especially in connection with the milestones of our lives, the celebrations of births, deaths or marriages. For centuries, they were visual symbols of nuanced messages in the language of flowers, or floriography, which the Victorians in particular excelled at. Plants have always been closely connected with the arts, featured in botanical illustration, in science as the playground of hybridisers or in fashion where flowers and their colours have been appropriated for the catwalk.

But how often do we stop and think about how these plants came to be here and why? What is their story? Because we all have a story to tell ourselves. Plants are no different. Here, I have attempted to highlight some of the unsung heroes of our gardens, avoiding the usual suspects, and I have attempted to shed new light on them and bring them up to date, as in the case of Rosa 'John Ystumllyn' (see pages 164-167).

I would very much like you to get to know your plants and hopefully marvel at their journey into your little corner of the world. The uses of some of the plants in history may surprise you especially since many of them are now grown solely for ornamental purposes. The majority of the plants we think so fondly of in our gardens appeared in the early herbals and medicinal writings for curing a range of ailments. Who would have imagined that the delicate *Nigella damascena* would help to banish nits (see pages 140-143)?

The plethora of common, vernacular or country names might make people realise just how vital botanical names can be. But it also raises the point that common names are just as useful in discovering the original uses of the plant, such as the likes of *Bergenia crassifolia*, commonly called Siberian tea as it can be used as a beverage (see pages 22-23). In reality, a plant may have several names, depending on which part of the world you reside in.

The curiosity of collectors, nurserymen, plant breeders and hybridists inspired them to experiment with each new influx of botanical treasures. Inevitably some popular flowers fell by the wayside becoming victims of the latest fads, as the beau monde strived for the next marvel to adorn their hothouses and boast about.

These new hybrids, whether manipulated or a result of natural crosses, tended to be more vigorous, with better colour variation and proved generally more desirable to audiences. As a result, the original species became increasingly hard to come by as they fell out of favour, often only to be found in specialist nurseries or dedicated plantsmens' gardens.

Eagle-eyed people like Marion Cran, Gertrude Jekyll and Clarence Elliott highlighted the importance of plucking flowers from near obscurity when the opportunity arises, because in every old garden there is a plant waiting to be rediscovered, to be revived and seen with new eyes. The ephemerality of gardens and in turn plants constantly make them vulnerable.

Just as now, historically the best way people preserved a previously unknown species was to distribute it to several garden owners, thus giving the plant a better chance of survival, each recipient using different methods of cultivation. Some plants were never offered commercially, instead being distributed among gardeners. They would often be forgotten when the gardener passed away, with no one there to remember the plant's provenance let alone its name if it ever had one.

Some newly introduced plants arrived only to disappear again; but others flourished to such an extent that they have become seriously invasive. Just look at *Rhododendron ponticum* (see pages 158-161). Initially pampered to within an inch of its life, it is now the bane of every estate manager across the country and listed on Schedule 9 of the Wildlife and Countryside Act 1981, meaning it is an offence to plant or allow this species to grow in the wild.

A fascinating fact about our gardens, large or small, is that they are full of history. You may even be in possession of an 'antique' without even knowing it. If you happen to grow any of the flowers I have included, then please go out and have a good look at your plants – I am certain you will begin to see them in a completely different light. There are so many more stories to be discovered in our outdoor spaces, if we only continue to keep looking. *A Short History of Flowers* may help fill in some of the gaps.

THE PROGRESS OF LOVE

Hollyhock

Alcea rosea syn. Althaea rosea

The introduction of the stately hollyhock to Britain, a member of the mallow family, has been linked with intrepid Queen Eleanor (1241-90), wife of Edward I (1239-1308), who is said to have brought it back from the Holy Land, when they travelled there during the Crusades. This lends some credence to its common name of hollyhock – the religious connotation of 'Holy' with '*hoc*', the Anglo-Saxon word for mallow. The synonym '*Althaea*' comes from the Greek for healing. And, apart from its numerous medicinal properties, the hollyhock has come to be valued for its commercial and culinary properties.

By the fifteenth century, hollyhocks were a common sight in English cottage gardens, and the addition of seeds from China, in 1573, enhanced the existing selection of plants to produce large double flowers. On observing these exuberant flowers, the herbalist, writer and gardener John Gerard (see page 87) called the hollyhock the 'outlandish rose'.

Hollyhocks bring us joy each summer and are forever associated with the quintessentially English cottage garden, and they have been a favourite subject for artists over the centuries. In the eighteenth century, French rococo painter Jean-Honoré Fragonard (1732-1806) famously captured the beauty of the flower, known as '*rose d'outremer*' or 'rose from beyond the sea'. Fragonard excelled at floral outdoor pastoral scenes, celebrated for their playfulness and often sensual hidden symbolism. His reputation for subtle nuances when depicting love scenes won him many admirers and, in 1770, he was commissioned by Louis XV's mistress Madame Du Barry (1743-93), to paint four large canvases for her new classical pavilion, set in the parkland at the Château de Louveciennes, about twenty miles from Paris.

The paintings, collectively known as *The Progress of Love* (*The Pursuit, The Meeting, The Lover Crowned* and *Love Letters*) depicted the courtship of two young lovers and the last, *Love Letters*, features an abundance of hollyhocks. It shows a woman seated on a pedestal, a small Spaniel nestled at its base, a pile of letters beside her, as a man leans into her, his head on her shoulder. The colour pink is very much associated with the rococo period in France, and the couple are framed by luscious pink hollyhocks. This all plays into Fragonard's discreet symbolism. In the language of flowers, the hollyhock symbolises abundance and fertility but also fidelity, just as dogs are traditional symbols of loyalty. This fourth tableau appears to be a reflection of the couple's mature love, perhaps reliving their courtship through their intimate correspondence which has led to the progression of their love.

The four paintings were hung in the Louveciennes Pavilion for a short time before Madame Du Barry inexplicably rejected and returned them to Fragonard. By 1789, the *Ancien Régime* was on the way out, with rumblings of the forthcoming revolution. Fragonard and his family returned to his home town of Grasse in southern France, and took up residence at his cousin's home, the Villa Maubert. The four canvases, which had been relegated to storage in the Louvre were moved to Grasse and displayed in the salon.

While resident at Grasse, Fragonard produced another ten paintings to complement *The Progress of Love*, including four long, thin panels depicting tall spires of creamy white and dark centred hollyhocks set behind ornate railings. This same railing can be seen in *The Lover Crowned*, holding back

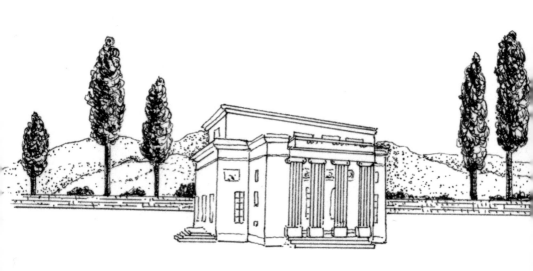

a rampant rose behind the couple. The ten canvases interspersed with the hollyhock panels were displayed in a way that probably echoed the garden views which had surrounded the Louveciennes Pavilion. According to novelist Alan Hollinghurst, Fragonard managed to create 'an extraordinary pictorial space, bringing the fragrant garden of the house indoors'.

Fragonard died peacefully in Paris in 1806, his remarkable paintings remaining mostly unseen at the Villa Maubert, in private hands until 1898, when the last member of the family had copies made (which still remain in the villa) before selling the fourteen original canvases.

In the more than 120 years since the paintings left Grasse, *The Progress of Love* cycle and its ten accompanying pieces have resided in a 'Fragonard Room' in different locations around the world. In 1916, the paintings were acquired by the Frick Collection in New York. Sadly, though, three of the hollyhock canvases were placed into storage. The remaining panel hung in a corner of the new Fragonard Room, where it was frequently obscured by an open door. Finally, in 2021, after just over a century apart, the missing panels finally came out of storage and were reunited with the rest of the collection.

Although far removed from their original idyllic French garden surroundings, at the Frick, the Fragonard Room has three large windows that overlook the gardens, which then leads the eye to the trees beyond in Central Park. At last, *The Progress of Love* is complete, with the hollyhocks standing guard between the canvases, just as Fragonard had envisaged all those years ago.

A LAID-BACK PLANT

Peruvian lily

Alstroemeria 'Indian summer'

*A*lstroemeria 'Indian summer' has the most attractive dark green bronzed foliage which contrasts beautifully with the flame-like yellow, red and orange flowers. If you already grow any kind of *alstroemeria*, take a good look at your plants. Yes, the leaves are 'upside down'.

Alstroemerias are not entirely unique in this behaviour – in which the petiole, or leaf stalk, as it grows, twists 180 degrees to invert the leaf so that the upper surface is actually the lower one. If you bend and secure a young shoot downwards, the leaf will make a second twist to show the same side. For many years, botanists have been scratching their heads over this behaviour. No one has been able to explain in layman's terms the reason behind it. In botany, this characteristic is known as 'resupination', or having resupinate leaves, the word originating from the Latin word *resupinus* – also the root of 'supine', or lying flat on your back.

The genus *Alstroemeria* commemorates the Swedish naturalist Baron Clas Alströmer (1736-94) who travelled throughout southern Europe studying sheep breeding. Alströmer had been a pupil of Professor Carl Linnaeus (see page 153) at Uppsala University. He later became one of the academic's 'apostles'; these were promising students Linnaeus recruited to travel the world and investigate, illustrate, collect and send back botanical specimens. He named plant genera after them as a reward.

In 1753, while at the home of the Swedish consul in Cádiz, in south-west Spain, Alströmer came across the Peruvian lily, which had been introduced to Spain via South America. Alströmer sent several of the fleshy roots back to Linnaeus. When the seedlings emerged, Linnaeus was so anxious to preserve them, he kept them in his bedchamber. He called the plant *Alstroemeria pelegrina*.

Over the years, the arrival of new species from South America, in particular the Andes, increased the material for hybridisation and selection. This has further resulted in a range of striking garden plants, such as *A.* 'Indian Summer' – a cultivar of the common orange *A. autantiaca*, introduced in 1831 from Chile.

Alstroemerias make fabulous cut flowers, with a long vase life, known in the florist trade, rather morbidly, as the 'art of a good slow death'.

CLOAKED IN MYSTERY

Poppy anemone

Anemone coronaria

'So full of variety and so dainty, so pleasant and so delightsome,' and 'is of its selfe alone almost sufficient to furnish a garden' - was how Parkinson (see page 133) glowingly praised the attributes of *Anemone coronaria* in 1629. In the gardening world, then as now, generosity is generally the unwritten rule where plants, seeds and cuttings of unusual or particularly lovely specimens change hands, between connoisseurs and amateurs. In many ways, this kindness had a practicality about it. Historically, when new plants arrived from far-flung places, nobody had a clue as to how to cultivate them and so it was deemed prudent to 'share' the spoils in case your specimen died; then all was not lost.

Regretfully, not everyone was inclined to share their prized flowers in this manner. Through the writings of Noël-Antoine Pluche (1688-1761), a French priest and educator, we hear the tale of a most ungenerous collector of the anemone. Between 1732 and 1750, he produced the illustrated, eight-volume *Spectacle de la Nature*; or *Nature displayed, being Discourses on such Particulars of Natural History*. Using a selection of fictional characters in various settings, he conveyed factual information on a wide range of topics about the natural world, history and life.

In the section entitled 'Of Flowers', Pluche tells of a famous florist and most diligent herbalist Monsieur Bachelier from Paris who had acquired a handsome collection of the best anemones from the East, most likely the Levant. It turned out that M. Bachelier was not one for sharing these beautiful blooms and for more than ten years he kept the anemones to himself, not a single seed or root allowed to pass into other people's hands.

On hearing about the florist's lack of generosity, one French parliamentary official became unhappy at this state of affairs, insisting that the flowers were the work of nature and should therefore be shared with everyone. So, dressed in his full official fur-trimmed attire, he visited M. Bachelier's country house knowing that the anemones would have set seed. As he walked through the man's garden, he 'accidentally' dropped his robe among the flowers. The councillor's manservant, who had been primed to this impending subterfuge, immediately stepped forward, scooped up his master's robe, which now harboured a quantity of the soft and downy seeds, folded it and promptly took it away. The plants derived from the 'liberated' seeds were abundantly shared among the councillor's friends, who grew them in their Paris gardens and ensured their further distribution far and wide. Oh, to be a fly on the wall of M. Bachelier's parlour when he discovered the councillor's underhand activities.

The flower took the rest of Europe by storm and for many years its star burned brightly as it took its place among other leading florists' flowers. There is no firm date on the arrival of *A. coronaria* into Britain, but by 1805 the passion for them was said to be in decline, as other novel flowers made their debuts and caught the gardener's imagination.

It was not until the early 1880s that interest in the flower was revived once more and this was down to Mrs Alice Lawrenson (1841–1900; née Bland) of Howth, Dublin, who diligently bred and selected the double and semi-double forms known as *Anemone coronaria* 'St Brigid'. This strain was described as having brightly coloured peony-like flowers.

A. coronaria flowers come in a range of colours but the blue is particularly stunning in both the single and double form. Bizarrely, the secrecy of M. Bachelier and the cloak and dagger behaviour of the French councillor seems to have followed the charming *A. coronaria* across the English Channel and over the Irish Sea. Alice Lawrenson, a regular contributor to *The Garden* and *The Gardeners' Chronicle*, hid behind the 'St Brigid' alias in order to avoid the publicity of being the gardener who had bred and raised the much-vaunted anemones. When she died, *The Gardeners' Chronicle* acknowledged in her obituary that, 'By many she was better known by her *nom de plume* of "St Brigid" than by her own name'; Lawrenson belonged to a plant exchange network that included the National Botanic Gardens at Glasnevin, Dublin, where she routinely donated the seeds of her anemones. The miserly M. Bachelier could have learnt some valuable lessons, indeed, from such a generous soul.

19

A CHARISMATIC CHARMER

Snapdragon

Antirrhinum majus

O ften snapdragons conjure fond memories of pinching the sides of
the flower together to make the muzzle-like 'jaws' of the 'dragon'
snap open and shut. Similar to lupins, snapdragons are heavily
reliant on bumble bees for their pollination because they possess the weight
needed to 'open' the mouth when they land on the lower lip of the flower.
Snapdragons, which come in a range of fantastic and vibrant colours, are
often considered rustic and filled with nostalgia as they ooze that contented
cottage garden feel.

Delving into the rich folklore of the flower, a darker side to them begins
to emerge. Their dried seed capsules resemble skulls and Gerard, perceptive
as ever, picked up on its macabre appearance in his 1597 *Herball*, noting
that: 'The seed is black, contained in husks ... in my opinion it is more like
unto the bones of a sheep's head.' Perhaps this goes some way to explain the
reason for the snapdragon's deeply rooted connection to necromancy.

In lore, snapdragons were considered to have supernatural properties,
possessing the power to protect a person against being poisoned, or
reflecting any curses back to the perpetrator when the flowers were
positioned in front of a mirror. At the height of the Renaissance, new powers
were bestowed upon the humble snapdragon. If you ever found yourself
short on charm, it was believed wearing the flower about your person could
miraculously enhance your social standing, as the flowers were said to give
you charisma. Well, there we are then!

While the efficacy of these charms is perhaps questionable, for the
modern fashionista the snappy flower character of the single varieties known
as the traditional 'mouth' types can be worn as clip-on earrings.

Predictably, over the years breeders have managed to produce
double-flowered snapdragons. These new 'open face', or 'butterfly', types
are really very beautiful, however, they no longer have the hinge to make
them 'snap'.

A WINTER'S BREW

Siberian tea

Bergenia crassifolia syn. *Saxifraga crassifolia* and *Megasea crassifolia*

The history of *Bergenia crassifolia* is a classic example of how a plant once removed from its natural habitat can lose its original identity and purpose. The leaves of *B. crassifolia* have traditionally been used to make Siberian tea, a refreshing caffeine-free drink, but in Europe the plant has become an indispensable addition to the garden, especially in winter.

B. crassifolia was first collected and described in Siberia by the German naturalist and ethnographer Johann Georg Gmelin (1709-55). While serving as a Russian naval officer on Vitus Bering's Second Kamchatka Expedition (Great Northern Expedition) of 1733-43, Gmelin gathered the research that would later form the foundation of his four-volume publication, *Flora Sibirica*, completed posthumously in 1769.

Linnaeus received Gmelin's plant in 1760 from St Petersburg and called it *Saxifraga crassifolia*. A Linnaean 'apostle', Dr Daniel Solander, introduced the plant into Britain in 1765, when he arrived in London. In 1794, a new genus, *Bergenia*, was created by the German botanist Conrad Moench (1744-1805) in memory of the anatomist Karl August von Bergen. The species name of *Crassifolia* comes from the Latin *crassus* meaning solid or thick, obviously alluding to the plant's dense leathery foliage; it is these distinctive leaves that give cause for its common name of Siberian tea.

The young green leaves are extremely bitter, with high levels of tannins. A natural fermentation process occurs throughout the winter months, reducing the amounts of tannins and after one winter they become brown, after two, black. The blackened leaves are harvested in spring and are ideal for making the brew, also called Chigir or Chigirsky tea, and is said to be reminiscent of pine nuts. In the European garden, the brown or blackened leaves are discarded.

Gertrude Jekyll (see page 195) was a huge fan of bergenias, which she used for edging borders and underplanting her shrubberies. In her 1899 publication, *Wood and Garden*, she wrote, 'I am never tired of admiring the fine solid foliage of this family of plants remaining, as it does, in beauty both winter and summer.'

A DISCOVERY IN DISGUISE

Bougainvillea

Bougainvillea spectabilis

*B*ougainvillea spectabilis has become synonymous with an unabashed flamboyancy: it demands your attention, unlike, perhaps, the person who originally brought it back to Europe. The plant's beauty lies not in its tubular flowers, but in the blousy colours of the papery bracts that surround them.

The often-told story of how the bougainvillea got its name, which we'll get onto shortly, goes hand in hand with the lesser-known tale of the first woman to circumnavigate the globe, said to be an herb woman with an extensive knowledge of plants and their medicinal properties.

The life of Jeanne Baret (1740-1807) is steeped in mystery. Certainly by the 1860s, she was living in Paris with the man who was to change her life immeasurably, the eccentric and self-absorbed French naturalist Philibert Commerçon (1727-73). In 1766, Commerçon joined the first French expedition to circumnavigate the globe as the ship's doctor and naturalist under the command of the debonair Louis Antoine de Bougainville (1729-1811). During the proposed three-year expedition, Commerçon was to sail on the *Etoile* with Bougainville on its sister ship, the *Boudeuse*.

Not to be left behind and ignoring the prohibition of women aboard the King's ships, Baret bound her breasts with strips of linen beneath loose-fitting men's clothes and quietly slipped on board the *Etoile* just minutes before it sailed. Was Commerçon part of the charade? Certainly, he noted in his journal, '... they have given me a valet named "Jean" Baret!'

Sharing a spacious cabin with Commerçon afforded Baret a small degree of privacy away from the 117 crew. And it seems any initial suspicions of her gender were allayed by her claims of being a eunuch.

In June 1767, the *Etoile* joined the *Boudeuse* in Rio de Janeiro. It was during this stop that Baret and Commerçon collected a variety of plant specimens, including a rather eye-catching magenta-coloured scrambling climber. Commerçon described and labelled the specimen '*Buginvillaea*'. At each place the *Etoile* anchored, Baret and Commerçon searched for plants with potential commercial or medicinal value. Commerçon suffered frequent bouts of ill health, therefore it is entirely possible that Jeanne Baret, botanising on her own, collected many of the thousands of plant specimens obtained during the Bougainville expedition.

Suspicion reared its head now and then about her gender, the men noting how 'Jean' never grew any facial hair nor undressed or relieved himself in front of them. She even managed to navigate her way, probably with the aid of Commerçon, through the 'baptism on the line' ceremony for a sailor's first crossing of the Equator, which involved being stripped and drenched with sea water. There had been near misses, of course, but it was only in early 1768, almost eighteen months into the voyage, that Baret's true identity was revealed.

Several people on the voyage kept journals, including Bougainville himself. This has led to contradictory versions of how and where Baret was finally discovered. Once exposed, Baret confessed to Bougainville that she had initially deceived Commerçon, thus avoiding implicating him.

In December, eight months after her exposure, the *Etoile* reached the Île de France (Mauritius). Commerçon became very ill and was unable to continue the journey. Baret remained with him at Port Louis as the Bougainville expedition headed home to France. Commerçon died in early 1773, leaving Baret almost destitute, except for around forty boxes of specimens. Baret reverted to dressing as a female and, in May 1774, married a French soldier, Jean Dubernat, ensuring her a safe passage back home. Just as she had quietly slipped on to the *Etoile* nine years earlier, so too did she unobtrusively walk down the gangplank onto French soil in 1775, to become the first woman to circumnavigate the globe.

Fourteen years after Baret's return, the French botanist Antoine Laurent de Jussieu (1748-1836) described the genus 'Buginvillaea'. A note in Commerçon's handwriting read, 'no plant with this character has been reported, we are allowed to give to the newly founded genus a new name and derive it from the most famous Mr de Bougainville, someone who appreciates all fields of natural history, the arts and sciences'. What is interesting is the use of 'we' in Commerçon's labelling. By 1799, the name *Bougainvillea spectabilis* had been validly published by Professor Carl Ludwig Willdenow (1765-1812). *Spectabilis* comes from the Latin for 'admirable' or 'remarkable', words which could easily apply to Jeanne Baret.

Baret was awarded a state pension in recognition of her contributions during the Bougainville expedition. This generosity appears to have been endorsed by Bougainville himself, who, in 1785, wrote of Baret's strength, courage and botanical expertise. Baret died twenty-two years later, on 5 August 1807, at the age of sixty-seven.

Over 250 years later, in 2012, Baret was finally commemorated in a new species of nightshade, *Solanum baretiae*, a trailing vine with a variety of leaf shapes and petals, in a range of colours, from white to violet, with hints of yellow. The plant's contradictory features seem to echo the everchanging persona of Jeanne Baret.

A SIDELINE IN PLANTS

Captain Rawes' camellia

Camellia reticulata 'Captain Rawes'

Over the years, people have always found innovative ways of supplementing their incomes. This was no different for the officials and ships' captains of the East India Company (EIC), an organisation active between 1600 to 1873. It had been formed to exploit trade, such as the highly prized commodity of tea, *Camellia sinensis*, between Europe, South Asia and the Far East.

Although their main cargo was tea, which took priority, there was always an interest in other potentially lucrative sidelines such as silks, paintings and plants, all carried in the company's ships, which were known as East Indiamen.

The journey from China via the Cape of Good Hope meant crossing the equator twice and live plants struggled to survive, exposed to salt water spray, fluctuating temperatures, vermin and a general lack of care. The high failure rate meant that plant specimens, like *Camellia reticulata*, that made it to London could not only command high prices but also a great deal of kudos for EIC officials.

Camellia reticulata is believed to have been collected by John Reeves (1774-1856), an amateur naturalist and inspector of tea for the EIC, also known for his collection of extremely fine drawings of Chinese plants and animals. Previously, Reeves had successfully introduced the Chinese wisteria to Europe. In 1816, he collected two specimens of *Wisteria sinensis* and, hedging his bets, sent one with Captain Welbank aboard the *Cuffnells*, and the other with Captain Richard Rawes (1784-1831) of the *Warren Hastings*. Both plants survived their subsequent journeys to Britain, which proved to be a very prosperous bet for all concerned.

Captain Rawes had already proved himself very capable of delivering healthy plants across the world and, in 1820, he brought Reeves' *C. Reticulata* from Whampoa, Canton (Guangzhou) to England. The plant produced large semi-double, rose-pink flowers for the first time in 1826 at the home of Rawes' sister, Elizabeth, and her husband Thomas Carey Palmer in Bromley. It was named after the good captain.

C. reticulata 'Captain Rawes' is now sold as a rare and historic specimen, as it appears to be quite difficult to propagate.

MUSIC TO THE EARS

Indian shot

Canna indica

Cannas, no matter where you see them, always exude an air of exoticism. Native to the tropical Americas, they were an early introduction into Europe around 1500, imported via the West indies into Spain and Portugal.

The Flemish physician Carolus Clusius (1526-1609), also known as Charles de l'Ecluse, the imperial gardener to Emperor Maximilian II, saw cannas growing in a garden in Lisbon and remarked on the use of *caña de cuentas*, or 'beaded cane' seeds, and their remarkable durability as rosary beads. Clusius wrote in 1601 of a plant named *Canna indica* - or *Flos Cancri*, as the closed flowers resembled a crab claw (*cancri* referring to the astrological symbol of Cancer as represented by a crab). Clusius also noted that the plant was generally cultivated in pots and had to be sheltered in a warm place to survive European winters.

By 1629, Parkinson was growing the *Canna* as the 'Indian flowering reede', and described two sorts, one red and the other yellow, with 'blacke seede, of a bignesse of pease'. *C. indica* appears to have then languished in relative obscurity, possibly due to its tenderness, until Théodore Année, the French consul general at Valparaíso, Chile, returned to France in 1846, with several plants. When he retired, he devoted his time to breeding cannas, the results of which led to the plant taking France by storm a few years later. By 1861, thousands of cannas were being grown in the squares of Paris, as the trend for tropical and sub-tropical plants increased.

While attending the Paris Exposition Universelle of 1867, the horticultural writer and gardener William Robinson (1838-1935) saw how extensively they were being used within the city's parks and became quite enamoured with them. Robinson encouraged their use on his return to Britain, where their large and beautiful bronzed foliage became prized as much as their brightly coloured flowers. As hardier species of *Canna* began to arrive into Europe, they could be found everywhere and as always with such popularity, the words 'common' and 'a bit brash' were not far behind. *C. indica* and its cousins thus soon tumbled from grace.

In their native habitat of South America, every part of *C. indica* has commercial value, whether it's for the flour made from its starchy rhizomes, the young leaves as a vegetable or for a combination of medicinal purposes. But it is the round hard black seeds that probably have the most entertaining and aesthetic uses. When boiled, the seeds produce a purple dye. A necklace discovered in an Argentinian tomb made of walnut shells containing *C. indica* seeds approximately 550 years old, demonstrates their extraordinary longevity as well. The plant's common name, Indian shot, is said to derive from a time during the Indian Rebellion of 1857, when soldiers, having run out of lead shot ammunition resorted to using the perfectly round and rock-hard seeds of *Canna indica*.

A far more enjoyable use for the seeds is in traditional musical instruments in various countries where the plants have migrated over the centuries. There is the *kayamb* or *kayamb*, a flat rattle shaken horizontally, which is used in Mauritius and the Mascarene Islands and several African countries, most commonly. The instrument is made of sugar cane flower stems or reeds filled with *Canna* seeds.

In my home country of Zimbabwe, where music has played a prominent role in the social, political and religious life of its communities, one of the most important instruments is the *hosho*. These are made from a hollowed-out gourd part-filled with the seeds of *C. indica*, which are called *hota*. Often boiled in salted water to improve its solidity, the gourd's flesh is scraped out before the *hota* are added. Sometimes, a simple pattern of small holes may be burned into gourd, but in many cases a more elaborate design is applied using a bradawl, or similar hand tool, before the instrument is sealed. The *hosho* come in pairs and are considered the heartbeat of an ensemble, as they are essential in keeping the pace of the music. The use of the *hosho* is said to light your way.

The revival of cannas in recent times has been astonishing, gracing our herbaceous borders and ornamental pots in abundance. Also, due to their lack of hardiness, they are perfect candidates for indoor plants. With the rise of indoor gardening and the increased fashion of houseplants, *C. indica* and its cultivars have been embraced by Millennials and Generation Z, thus making it more popular than ever.

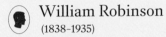

William Robinson
(1838-1935)

Irish horticulturist, publisher and author William Robinson held some very firm views on plants and gardens. He is one of the most significant but quarrelsome figures in garden history and abhorred formality in gardening practices – such as topiary and exotic bedding schemes – instead favouring hardy perennials planted in a more naturalistic style. As the horticultural correspondent for *The Times*, he covered the Great Exhibition in Paris in 1867, where he found botanical inspiration for some of his books. In 1870, he published *The Wild Garden*, followed, in 1883, by *The English Flower Garden*, which has been described as 'the most widely read and influential gardening book ever written'. Back in 1871, Robinson launched his weekly journal, *The Garden*, which enabled him to reach a wider audience for the ideas he put into practice in the 1,000 acres at Gravetye Manor, Sussex, his home from August 1885 until his death in 1935.

SPEND! SPEND! SPEND!

Chinese plumbago

Ceratostigma willmottianum

*C*eratostigma willmottianum is a striking shrub with cobalt blue flowers and contrasting autumnal red leaves. Its name celebrates Ellen Willmott (1858-1934), one of the most successful British horticulturalists of the late nineteenth and early twentieth centuries. Willmott's devotion to her plants eventually led her to bankruptcy, after she spent her way through a vast fortune.

Driven by a compulsion to acquire new plants to grow and improve, Willmott organised, financed or co-sponsored plant-hunting expeditions, some of which she joined herself. Her endeavours resulted in about 200 new species and cultivars being named after her, or associated with her through her celebrated garden at Warley Place, Essex.

Willmott benefitted from the exploits of the British plant collector Ernest Wilson (1876-1930), who had conducted two trips to China. In 1906, Wilson was approached by Charles Sargent of the Arnold Arboretum in Boston to make a return trip to the country. Having just become a father, Wilson was reluctant to go. Sargent wrote to Willmott in the hope that she could persuade the botanist. Willmott pledged £200, which she probably couldn't afford, and reportedly persuaded Wilson to change his mind. The expedition resulted in his collection of *C. willmottianum* seeds in the Min River valley, Sichuan Province, in 1908. Seeds were sent to several people, but Willmott was the only one who succeeded in raising two plants, one was planted at Warley, the other at Spetchley Park, Worcestershire, the home of her beloved sister Rose. *C. willmottianum* was later described at the Royal Botanic Gardens, Kew by the Austrian-born taxonomist Otto Stapf in 1914.

Alongside Gertrude Jekyll, Willmott was one of only two women nominated for the Royal Horticultural Society's prestigious Victoria Medal of Honour in 1897. Alas, she did not turn up to receive it. The reason is heart-breaking, yet may go some way to explaining her later reputation for being 'difficult': Georgiana Tufnell, whom Willmott was in love with, was due to marry Lord Mount Stephen the next day. Difficult or not, Willmott's dedication to horticulture can never be underestimated.

ROYAL SEAL OF APPROVAL

Rose bay willowherb, Fireweed

Chamaenerion angustifolium syn. *Epilobium angustifolium*

I n his 1597 book *Herball*, John Gerard (see page 87) praised the singular beauty of *Chamaenerion angustifolium*, which he said had 'leaves like willow ... garnished with brave flowers of great beautie, of an orient purple colour, which do grow in my garden very goodly to behold'. It took another thirty years before John Parkinson (see page 133) noted the plant's antisocial tendencies to 'spring againe in many places farre asunder'. Other growers accused the plant of 'licentious and ungovernable' creeping before it was banished to the kitchen garden, where in spring the young and tender shoots were harvested and steamed like asparagus.

C. angustifolium appears to be one of those plants that insinuated itself into many countries over the centuries before happily setting up home in domestic gardens. It was originally introduced to gardeners under the name of French Willow, Parkinson called it 'the Willowe flower' and, before gardeners knew better, it was considered a rarity and a prized garden flower.

The documentation and publication of a region's flora has been in practice for hundreds of years. In Denmark, this was instigated in 1761 and eventually completed in 1833 to produce the *Flora Danica*, or the Flora of Denmark. The 17-volume publication included 3,240 colour and part colour plates of botanically accurate plants all hand-painted from life by a series of Denmark's most talented botanical artists. The plants were depicted in flower often including their root system. *C. angustifolium* was one of the earliest inclusions in the *Flora Danica*, appearing in the second volume produced between 1765 and 1766.

The German botanist Georg Christian Oeder (1728–91) was instrumental in the initiation and publication of the *Flora Danica* project. He travelled extensively, collecting and documenting plants including *C. angustifolium*. One contemporary account recorded how the local people 'were amazed to see a fine educated man like him creeping about in the mountains looking for herbs'. Oh, the irony – Parkinson would have smiled.

The *Flora Danica* was a momentous undertaking, one worthy of commemoration. So when, in 1790, Crown Prince Frederick ordered the manufacture of a dinner service, the manager of the Royal Porcelain Factory of Copenhagen, Johan Theodor Holmskjold, suggested a *Flora Danica*-inspired service. The state-funded initiative was to recreate the beautiful colour illustrations upon an exquisite hand-painted porcelain collection like no other. It was rumoured the service had been a placatory gesture to Catherine the Great (1729–96), who died before its completion.

In 1802, with one hundred plate settings completed, production was halted, however. It was later resumed in 1862 as a wedding gift for Denmark's Princess Alexandra on her marriage, in 1863, to the Prince of Wales, the future Edward VII. *C. angustifolium* was depicted in the Copenhagen *Flora Danica* service under its synonym *Epilobium angustifolium* on a gorgeous reticulate-edged dessert plate.

Over the years *C. angustifolium's* reputation has suffered, in part due to its habit of spreading via underground rhizomes, but also because of its ability to produce thousands of seeds per plant each year. It was also discovered during the Second World War that *C. angustifolium* was a very successful pioneer species that thrived on burnt ground and rapidly colonised bombed sites, hence the other common names of fireweed or bomb weed.

This 'licentious and ungovernable' behaviour has resulted in most gardeners now giving this still beautiful magenta-flowered plant a very wide berth. Therefore, may I recommend instead its sister plant, the much better-behaved *C. angustifolium* 'Album', with glorious spires of snow-white flowers and the delicate pink form of *C. angustifolium* 'Stahl Rose'.

PERENNIAL GENEROSITY

Glory-of-the-snow

Chionodoxa luciliae syn. *Scilla luciliae*

Chionodoxa luciliae is a lovely clear blue, spring flowering bulb commonly known as glory-of-the-snow because it often flowers while there is still snow on the ground.

According to J. G. Baker, in the 1879 *Curtis's Botanical Magazine*, *C. luciliae* was introduced into cultivation by George Maw in May 1877 after obtaining specimens while ascending the Nymph Dagh, east of Smyrnia (modern day Izmir in western Turkey). Maw (1832–1912) was a geologist, botanist and ceramicist, probably best known for his 1886 monograph on the genus *Crocus*, as well as the beautiful decorative encaustic clay tiles that he and younger brother Arthur manufactured at their company, Maw & Co. of Broseley, Shropshire. The botanically accurate floral designs were inspired by Maw's interests. He also established a well-known garden during his long-term tenancy, from 1853 to 1886, at Benthall Hall, Shropshire, today a National Trust property.

C. luciliae was first recorded and described by the Swiss botanist Pierre Edmond Boissier (1810–85) in 1844. Boissier grew up with a fascination for the natural world, having spent much of his childhood exploring the Jura mountains and the Alps. Along with an interest in botany, he inherited a fortune large enough that he could have pursued a life of leisure, instead of dedicating his life to travelling across Europe, North Africa and western Asia, collecting and documenting plants. As a result, Boissier became one of the most prolific plant collectors of the nineteenth century, although his name is now rarely mentioned.

Bossier married in 1840 and was often accompanied on his expeditions by his beautiful wife, Lucile, (née Butini-de la Rive; 1822–49), also a very knowledgeable naturalist. The Boissiers travelled to the Orient, Middle East and North Africa in search of new plants. Boissier absolutely adored his wife and often gave the specific 'luciliae' to some species they discovered. He was especially fascinated by Lucile's sky-blue eyes, so when Boissier came across a plant with delicate blue star-shaped blooms amid the melting snow of the Bozdağ Mountains, in western Turkey, there was no doubt about what to name it. It was officially acknowledged as *Chionodoxa luciliae* in 1842.

Tragically, in 1849, while touring with her husband in Spain and Algeria, Lucile contracted typhoid fever and died in Granada, at the age of 27. Boissier was devastated – indeed, after his death it was reported how the poor bereft man had lived the rest of his life 'in the shadows of his sorrow'. However, through their work together and Boissier's own botanical discoveries, Lucile's name survives as a perennial testimony to their love.

When George Maw first encountered C. luciliae he remarked that it was 'one of the most sumptuous displays of floral beauty I ever beheld'.

Maw was a most generous and benevolent person who not only introduced C. luciliae to the gardening community, but after sharing the plant with his friends, devoted the money received from the sale of surplus stock to the funds of the Gardeners' Benevolent Institution (later the Gardeners' Royal Benevolent Society, now better known as Perennial).

The charity had been founded in 1839, its main aim to provide a source of income to gardeners, in particular head gardeners, who in their retirement often lost their tied property at the end of their careers and were in danger of becoming destitute. The charity garnered much support from the public – even author Charles Dickens appeared as a keynote speaker at the annual fundraising dinner. When Maw made his donations, the focus of the charity was shifting to providing accommodation for ageing gardeners, a care home and retirement housing. Over 180 years later, Perennial as a charity goes from strength to strength.

At Benthall Hall, the gardens Maw created were adapted to showcase and trial many new plants, including his beloved crocuses, which he and his fellow botanists collected. Maw's glory-of-the-snow proved itself to be perfectly hardy in the open ground at the stately home, and its bulbs, from 1877, not only increased in size but in number.

Maw honoured the Boissiers' lifelong commitment with *Crocus boissieri*. This was especially poignant given that Edmond and Lucile's daughter and botanist Caroline Barbey-Boissier (1847-1918), upheld her mother's legacy by accompanying her father on plant hunting expeditions after her mother's death.

At Benthall Hall, each year hundreds of visitors are able to appreciate Maw's chionodoxas, crocuses and other plants, still flourishing over 130 years after his death. If truth be told, C. luciliae can be a pest, but hey, it could be worse – they are still incredibly gorgeous, after all.

CURATIVE, COSMETIC AND CULINARY

Hoary rock-rose

Cistus incanus

In the 1930s, Sir Oscar Warburg of Epsom wrote about the scandalous way that the *Cistus* family had a 'frailty in their conception of marital relations'. This becomes all too apparent when you attempt to untangle the many species available. Most hail from the Mediterranean, and are a joy to have in any garden.

Today, the Royal Botanic Gardens, Kew has a host of scientific research centres and collections that would have stunned its founder Princess Augusta (1719-1772) were she living today. One such department is the Fungarium - yes, there is such a thing - where the importance of fungi as a provider of food and medicine, as well as their essential role in our ecosystems, is evident.

Part of fungi's success is its ability to interact with other species. One example is the mutual association between *Cistus incanus* and *Tuber melanosporum*, better known as Périgord truffle. *C. incanus* has the capacity to create a symbiotic relationship with it, enabling it to obtain nutrients that would otherwise be unavailable. This alliance was first identified in nature, then exploited in experiments with inoculated seedlings planted out in truffle orchards, or *truffières*. Consequently, quantities of Périgord truffles, which can command eye-watering prices, have been obtained from plantations where *Cistus incanus* has been planted among a range of oak trees (traditionally conducive to the enhancement of truffle growth). This modern form of 'trufficulture' means you can now purchase pre-inoculated pots of *C. incanus* and other 'truffle plants' from specialist nurseries.

The wide-ranging powers of *C. incanus* make it undoubtedly a great all-rounder. In ancient Greece, its properties caused arguments among the deities who gathered at Mount Olympus to decide which plants should possess which attributes. The gods thought *Cistus* ideal for healing the wounds of embattled warriors. However, the goddesses could only see the plant's beautifying qualities. Unable to agree, the plant was given both curative and cosmetic properties. With this relatively new scientific application and their power to stimulate the growth of the ultimate gastronomic fungi, *C. incanus* is undoubtedly a plant to be admired.

CHRISTIAN DIOR'S LUCKY CHARM

Lily of the valley

Convallaria majalis

W hen it comes to floral folklore, surely few flowers bring such good omens as the lily of the valley. Which is just as well because the French fashion designer Christian Dior (1905–57), chose lily of the valley as his favourite flower, muse and good luck charm, a devotion which he maintained throughout his life.

Lily of the valley is an ancient plant, which grows wild in most parts of Europe. Although every part of the plant is highly toxic, it was one of the earliest flowers to be brought into our gardens. Its heady scent has ensured its place in the affections of people for centuries.

As for its health benefits, in his 1530 publication *Herbarum vivae eicones*, the German theologian and botanist Otto Brunfels (1488–1534) noted that previous herbalists had been 'silent as fishes' regarding the plant's medicinal properties. However, in 1544, Renaissance physician Pietro Andrea Mattioli (honoured in the genus *Matthiola*) recorded that a pinch of lavender flowers and rosemary added to distilled water made from lily of the valley produced *Aqua aurea* or golden water. This highly prized solution was in such great demand it was kept in gold or silver vessels for use in the treatment of headaches, hysterical manifestations and faintings.

While there are numerous English common names for lily of the valley, my personal favourite is the Elizabethan 'lilliconfancie'. But one of the oldest is 'mugget', derived from the French '*muguet*'. The flower is so important in France it has its own annual festival, *La fête du muguet* or lily of the valley day, on 1 May. The tradition dates back to King Charles IX who was given *le muguet* on that day in 1561. He was so taken with it that each year, he presented bouquets of the flower to each of the ladies of his court and pronounced that from that day onwards it would be the official flower of 1 May.

It is not unusual for families to rise early on that day and go into the woods to gather the flowers in order to gift a sprig to their nearest and dearest to bring joy and good fortune for the year ahead – and most fittingly in the language of flowers, lily of the valley signifies the return of happiness. Equally popular on that day were the *bals de muguet* or lily of the valley dances, at which young single people would meet without parental supervision, the women dressed in white and the men with the flower in their buttonholes.

Christian Dior often wore the flower in his buttonhole just as his models sported outlandish *boutonnières* on the catwalk. In order to ensure that he had a constant supply of the flower, Dior's personal florist, Madame Paule Dedeban, grew it all year round in a heated glasshouse so that the designer was never without his spring bloom. Dior was well known for his superstitious nature, and his personal astrologer Madame Delahaye was tasked with choosing the most auspicious dates, always an even number, for the launch of new collections or in helping him make important decisions. Dior always carried an assortment of lucky charms, among them a piece of engraved gold, a little piece of wood, a four leaf clover and, of course, a stem of lily of the valley. In line with tradition, Dior gave the flower to all his clients and staff on the first day of May.

Dior's adoration of the flower inspired his designs and it appeared on fabric, both in printed and embroidered form. He used the shape of the leaves and flowers to embellish hats and jewellery.

In his autobiography, Dior wrote 'in the spring of 1954 I put forward the "Lily-of-the-Valley" line, inspired by my lucky flower, a line which was at once young, graceful, and simple'. Lily of the valley became the symbol of the House of Dior and *La Ligne Muguet* later inspired one of the designer's iconic perfumes, Diorissimo, in which the principal notes include his lucky charm. More recently in 2023, as a tribute to Monsieur Dior, the exquisite *Muguet* tableware collection was unveiled.

As an extra special touch, the fashion house's *'Les petite mains'*, or 'little hands', the highly skilled seamstresses who brought his designs to life, delicately incorporated a sprig of the flower into the hemlines of his couture dresses. The 'little hands' often appeared on the runway at the end of each fashion show.

Christian Dior died in October 1957, and at his funeral the following month, his coffin was covered in hot house lily of the valley. This would have been Madame Dedeban's final floral tribute to him – the flower that had always been to Dior a reminder of eternal spring.

THE SPIRITS OF HORSES

Cosmos

Cosmos bipinnatus

E very year, during March and April, for a few short weeks the spectacular sight of acres of *Cosmos bipinnatus* flowering up to 4 feet tall in Johannesburg's 260-acre Delta Park is truly remarkable. What is even more astonishing is the fact that cosmos is native to Mexico and South America. So how, and more to the point why, have they become such a celebrated attraction in South Africa?

The genus *Cosmos* was established in 1791 by the Spanish priest and botanist Antonio José Cavanilles (1745-1804), who had a garden famed for its exotic plants, including *C. bipinnatus*. Cosmos arrived in Britain from Madrid in 1798 but met with little success until the late nineteenth century when hybridists discovered its true potential.

At this time, over in South Africa, Britain's attempts to wrest control from the Boers, the Afrikaans-speaking farmers, of the land under their control initiated the start of the second Anglo–Boer War in 1899. While this was initially expected to be short-lived, it was not to be; the war lasted almost three years with the British encountering various problems. The stable-fed British horses were ill-equipped to cope with the region's alien environment. In contrast, the Boers rode small, indigenous Basuto ponies which were used to the terrain and happy to graze on the abundant but coarse veld grass. As the war progressed, the shortage of horses became a serious issue, and agents were sent to the United States, Argentina, Spain, Italy and Hungary to buy horses and mules.

As more horses arrived, a severe shortage of suitable fodder developed, and the British began to import feed from Argentina. Unbeknown to them, the bales harboured *Cosmos bipinnatus* seeds. These supplies were transported by rail and road into the continent's interior.

When the war ended in 1902, over 300,000 horses had perished – an unprecedented rate of loss. The most unlikely positive outcome from this conflict were the thousands of stowaway cosmos seeds that proceeded to germinate along the roads, railway lines and old battlefield sites. Since then, the flowers have flourished and now draw international tourists and photographers to Delta Park, the site of an early twentieth-century cattle farm, which explains the high concentration of *C. bipinnatus*.

A YOUNG MARTYR OF NATURAL HISTORY

Montbretia

Crocosmia x crocosmiiflora

The bright orange flowers of *Crocosmia*, which I am extremely fond of, have historically, for many gardeners, been a nightmare colour to place in a border – words such as 'vulgar' or even 'tasteless' being muttered as the pages of nursery catalogues were hastily turned. However, in recent years the popularity of the hot border planting style has redeemed these once derided flowers, and their fiery cousins, which now take pride of place next to vibrant yellow rudbeckias and sultry scarlet dahlias.

The pale orange *Crocosmia aurea* was first collected from South Africa around 1846 by German naturalist and explorer Wilhelm Peters (1815-83) who sent it to the Botanical Garden in Berlin. In the 1870s, George Honington Potts of Fettes Mount, Lasswade, near Edinburgh, received a consignment of plants from South Africa, including several corms that bore graceful spikes of bright orange flowers with reddish brown tips. A few years later, he generously distributed his plants among a variety of people and organisations, including Maximilian Leichtlin (1831-1910), a German horticulturalist and hybridiser from Baden-Baden. In 1877, this plant was given the name *Crocosmia pottsii*.

Three years later in August 1880, *The Garden Magazine* announced a new hybrid from the celebrated French nurseryman Victor Lemoine of Nancy. This was a cross between *Crocosmia pottsii* and *Crocosmia aurea*, and Lemoine proposed the name *Montbretia crocosmaeflora*. *Montbretia* was a generic blast from the past which had lain in botanical limbo for many years. It commemorated Antoine François Ernest Coquebert de Montbret (1781-1801), a talented French botanist and plant collector. From the age of twelve, he had studied natural history at the King's gardens, established as a medicinal garden in 1626. It was during this period that Montbret became firm friends with another budding botanist, Augustin Pyramus de Candolle (1778-1841) from Switzerland, who later gave us the word 'taxonomy'.

At seventeen, Montbret signed up as a naturalist's assistant within the scientific team due to accompany Napoleon Bonaparte (1769-1821) on his ill-fated Egyptian invasion in 1798. On arrival Montbret botanised, documenting the local flora before being appointed the first librarian of the

Institute of Egypt in Cairo, established by Napoleon. Montbret received
a letter from his father who wrote: 'I dream about the recognition you will
receive ... about the friends you will make for life.' Montbret responded, 'It
is not without risks that one can botanize here, and those who strive for the
title of "Martyrs of Natural History," could not find a more conducive place.'

Sadly, the risks were all too real, as in April 1801, at the tender age
of twenty, in the final days of their evacuation from Cairo, just as his
companions were boarding a ship to return home to France, he succumbed
to the Plague. The genus *Montbretia* was published in 1803 by de Candolle in
memory of his friend. It is unclear as to which plant de Candolle attributed
the name.

Lemoine's *Montbretia crocosmaeflora* proved very popular, with
a corm selling for around 6 francs – 'enough money for a good meal

at a fine restaurant'. In the meantime, he embarked on an extensive crossbreeding programme and finally settled on the new name of *Crocosmia x crocosmiiflora* – '*Crocosmia* crossed with flowers like *Crocosmia*', which indeed it is.

Although the generic name of *Montbretia* is now widely misapplied and has been long since abandoned and replaced with *Crocosmia*, for many people, like myself, it remains in everyday use. Naturally this goes some way in upholding the legacy of a most promising and eager young botanist.

FROM THE WORKHOUSE TO THE COUNTRY HOUSE

Pinks

Dianthus 'Mrs Sinkins'

What is the difference between pinks and carnations? This is a question frequently asked and rightly so, because of their similarities. The simple answer is that they derive from different species. Pinks are from the hybridisation of the Eastern European *Dianthus plumarius* and other *Dianthus* species, while the carnation was developed solely from *Dianthus caryophyllus*. The name *Dianthus* comes from the Greek words *dios* meaning divine and *anthos* for flower.

In the late sixteenth century, botanical writer and gardener John Gerard decided the leaves reminded him of deeply cut feathers and gave the plant the name of *plumarius* or 'feathered pink'. Although pinks, with their distinctive spicy clove-like scent, had been around since the twelfth century, they consistently fell in and out of fashion and were relegated to a supporting role in the garden. According to the horticulturalist John Rea (1605-77), they 'only serve to set the sides of borders in spacious gardens'.

It was not until after 1780 that pinks came into their own, when they were embraced by the florists' societies, joining tulips, anemones, carnations, hyacinths, polyanthus, ranunculus and auriculas as being highly prized.

The pink, like the other florists' flowers, was essentially a working man's plant, grown for leisure by miners in the north of England and the spinners and weavers of Paisley in Scotland. This working-class hobby was reflected in the prizes offered at the annual shows, which included garden forks, spades or trowels.

One such enthusiastic florist was John Sinkins, who, when he was not obsessing over his flowers, especially the pink, was the master of the Eton Union Workhouse in Slough, Berkshire. Sinkins' wife, Catherine (née Rowe), was the matron at the workhouse. In the late 1860s, he raised a deliciously scented double-fringed, white-flowered pink. Strictly speaking this would not have qualified as a florist's flower because it had a weak calyx that invariably bursts, losing the flower petal's uniformity and giving it an untidy but rather resplendent appearance. However, this was the beauty of this particular pink, which, with its intoxicating scent, brings to mind the lavish feather boa-covered costumes once worn by the dancers of the infamous Folies Bergère in 1930s Paris.

The word soon got out about the new exotic-looking flower and a local nurseryman, Charles Turner of the Royal Nurseries at Slough, also known as the 'king of florists', persuaded John Sinkins to sell him his stock. Sinkins had been toying with the idea of naming this new flower 'Queen Victoria', however, he had a change of heart and finally agreed to sell it on the condition that it would be named in honour of his own wife, *Dianthus* 'Mrs Sinkins'. It was first exhibited at the Royal Horticultural Society show in 1880 to great acclaim, and over the years *D*. 'Mrs Sinkins' has become a must-have plant in all the best grdens, seamlessly moving from the workhouse to the country house.

Catherine Sinkins died in 1917, her husband in 1926. Twelve years later, in 1938, the town of Slough became a borough and this status required a new coat of arms. The new armorial bearings of Slough appeared as 'a swan holding in its beak a white pink slipped and leaved'. The swan symbolised the county of Buckinghamshire before Slough was incorporated into Berkshire in 1974 and *D*. 'Mrs Sinkins' commemorated the region's extensive horticultural history.

Just imagine how delighted the Sinkins would have been had they known that their town would choose to honour their beautiful flower in such a manner.

Note on florists

As early as 1623, the word 'florist' was first used to
describe people who grew certain flowers purely for their
aesthetic qualities and then exhibited them at shows that
were known as 'florist's' or 'pink feasts', held in public
houses around the country. The only restriction on what a
florist could exhibit was that the plants were selected for
their beauty rather than utility. Interestingly, the florists'
flowers tended to be compact, like auriculas, and kept in
small terracotta pots on a windowsill, or plants that did
not require a great deal of space in a cottager's garden.
John Parkinson used the term 'florist' a number of times
in his 1629 *Paradisi*. However, the modern use refers to
people in the cut flower industry and was used in 1822
by botanist and influential horticultural journalist John
Claudius Loudon (1783–1843).

UNREQUITED LOYALTY

Wallflower

Erysimum cheiri syn. *Cheiranthus cheiri*

In 1829, William Cobbett (1763-1835) marvelled at how the wallflower 'grows well on old walls, or any walls, indeed on rubbish of any kind, and makes a pretty show wherever it is found'. The wallflower does indeed thrive on walls; the seeds are said to have arrived with the Caen limestone that William the Conqueror imported from Normandy to build his castles from 1066 onwards. The synonym *Cheiranthus*, meaning 'hand flower', is a more fitting name, as it was used in 'nose gays', small hand-held bouquets of fragrant flowers, held close to the nose to mask unwholesome odours (as wallflowers were likened to the scent of violets).

The Greek physician Pedanius Dioscorides (c.40-90 AD) noted that the yellow wallflower was best for medicinal use, and this was one of the first flowers Scottish botanical illustrator Elizabeth Blackwell (née Blachrie, 1707-58) depicted in 1737 with a detailed description of the flower's habits and medicinal properties.

In floriography *Erysimum cheiri* symbolises fidelity in misfortune. Well, Elizabeth soon learnt all about fidelity and misfortune. Her husband, Alexander, was an absolute scoundrel who dabbled in failed ventures, landing himself in a debtor's prison for two years. To support her family, Elizabeth compiled the beautifully illustrated *A Curious Herbal*, documenting the medicinal qualities of plants growing in London's Chelsea Physic Garden at that time. Between 1737 and 1739, and endorsed by the Royal College of Physicians, she published her work in weekly instalments, using 500 illustrations she had drawn, engraved and hand-coloured herself. The *Herbal* made enough money to liberate her husband. However, he promptly went back to his bad ways before running off to Sweden, only to be executed for conspiracy for interfering in the line of succession there in 1748.

Although Elizabeth's loyalty was never rewarded, her work was admired. An expanded German and Latin edition of her work, *Herbarium Blackwellianum Emendatum Et Auctum*, brought her to Linnaeus' attention, who affectionately referred to her as *Botanica Blackwellia* as if she were a plant. No doubt this would have given Elizabeth a degree of comfort.

PERFECT ARMS FOR AN AMERICAN DUCHESS

Californian poppy

Eschscholzia californica

When the early Spanish sailors, in the sixteenth century, first set eyes on the golden landscape of the Californian hillsides they exclaimed, '*Tierra del fuego!*' or Land of fire! This is where the barely pronounceable genus *Eschscholzia* grew so abundantly.

The plant's fiery, orange-coloured flowers earned the name '*copa del ora*', which means 'cup of gold', drawing on the legend that the orange gold petals of the *Eschscholzia californica* filled the soil with the same precious metal. No one could have anticipated just how prophetic this would be when the Californian Gold Rush came in the 1850s.

The Indigenous Peoples of California, however, were more interested in the plant's traditional medicinal and culinary properties which, among other things, was a mild sedative when boiled or steamed. The plants could be eaten as a green vegetable and the pollen used for cosmetic purposes.

In 1792, Archibald Menzies (1754-1842), ship's surgeon and naturalist on HMS *Discovery*, officially recorded the plant. Menzies, when not attending to the unpredictable and challenging health needs of the crew, collected plants for scientist, explorer and botanist Sir Joseph Banks (1743-1820). Menzies later brought seeds of the Californian poppy back to the Royal Botanic Gardens, Kew. The few plants grown from these seeds soon disappeared from cultivation and only remained in herbaria as dried specimens.

The next encounter with the plant was more than two decades later, in 1816, when the dashing German poet and botanist Aldelbert von Chamisso (1781-1838) travelled with the Russian Romanov discovery expedition to the Pacific coast. Chamisso collected the plant and later described and published an account of it, along with a life-size colour illustration. He named the genus in honour of his fellow passenger, Prussian naturalist Johann Friedrich Eschscholtz (1783-1831). It would seem that spelling was not Chamisso's forte as he omitted the 't'. Therefore, under those unyielding rules of botanical nomenclature, the genus *Eschscholzia* remains one of the most misspelt plant names to this day. In 1826, he reported that the seeds had not grown satisfactorily for him either.

It is down to the Scottish botanist David Douglas (see page 123), employed by the Horticultural Society of London (the Royal Horticultural Society), that *E. californica*, a plant previously only known to botanists, was introduced to a wider audience. When Douglas visited the region in the late 1820s, he was aware that Menzies had botanised in the area. Some of the elders among the local community recalled their encounters with Archibald Menzies, the 'red-faced man who cut off the limbs of men and gathered grass'.

E. californica finally got the recognition it deserved when, in 1903, it was officially designated the state flower of California. Centuries after the first European sighting of that golden haze along the western coastline, *Eschscholzia californica* made an unexpected appearance in British heraldry when, in 2018, Californian-born actress, activist and humanitarian Meghan Markle (1981–) married Prince Henry 'Harry' of Wales (1984–), fifth in line to the British throne.

As per tradition, a new coat of arms was granted and created as Meghan and Prince Harry assumed the titles of Duke and Duchess of Sussex. The Duchess' coat of arms reflects her heritage and interests, which can be seen on her half of the shield. The blue background represents the Pacific Ocean off the California coast, while the two golden rays across the shield are symbolic of the sunshine of the Duchess's home state. Below the shield, set in the grass, sits a row of *Eschscholzia californica*, symbolising the region's golden mineral wealth.

On her wedding day, Meghan, Duchess of Sussex, wore a 16 foot-long silk tulle veil, which was not only hand-embroidered with the distinctive national flowers of each of the 53 Commonwealth countries but also that of *Eschscholzia californica*.

As for the spelling, the writer and gardener James Shirley Hibberd (see page 101) wistfully remarked: 'Peace to his dust, honour to his memory, and may his name … be henceforth and for ever be spelt correctly.' Not a chance!

A HATBOX FIT FOR A PLANT

Mrs Robb's bonnet

Euphorbia amygdaloides var. *Robbiae* syn. *Euphorbia robbiae*

It is not often that you attend a wedding and come home with a new species of plant. But this is exactly what happened to Mrs Mary Anne Robb (née Boulton, 1829-1912), an English botanist and correspondent of the Royal Botanic Gardens, Kew.

She was the granddaughter of the eighteenth-century Birmingham manufacturer, engineer and foremost Lunar Society member Matthew Boulton (1728-1809), who was instrumental in the introduction of James Watt's pioneering steam engine; Robb certainly came from enterprising stock.

In 1891, Robb had travelled to Greece for a friend's wedding and took the opportunity to visit Turkey. On her way home, her carriage passed through a wooded area on the outskirts of Istanbul where she spotted the tall attractive inflorescence of a *Euphorbia*. She asked her guide to dig up the specimen, but with nowhere to put the newly uprooted plant, she promptly evicted her lavish wedding bonnet from its hatbox and carefully placed the plant inside for safe travel back to England.

The plant she collected was a wild species of *Euphorbia amygdaloides*, the common wood spurge. A perennial with evergreen, often red-tinged, leaves below yellowish-green flowers held in saucer-like bracts, Robb's newly acquired specimen had very striking yellow, acid-lime green bracts, which had initially caught her eye.

On her return home, Robb succeeded in cultivating her *Euphorbia*, which proved to be very good for ground cover, especially in dry shade. She shared it among her horticultural acquaintances, including Gertrude Jekyll and William Robinson. Another close friend and one of the greatest and most knowledgeable gardeners of his time, Edward Augustus 'Gussie' Bowles (1865-1954), had developed a much-admired garden at Myddleton House, Middlesex. When Gussie found out the manner by which the plant had arrived in England, he promptly gave it the moniker 'Mrs Robb's bonnet'.

Though this species was originally called *E. robbiae*, around 1975 it was accorded the varietal status of *E. amygdaloides* var. *Robbiae* 'Mrs Robb's bonnet'. No doubt Mrs R. would have been most gratified at this outcome.

GOLDEN BELLS IN A DELL

Forsythia

Forsythia x intermedia

The first species of forsythia to be described was *Forsythia suspensa* in Japan by Swedish botanist Carl Thunberg (1743-1828) who noticed a familial likeness and placed it under the genus *Syringa* in his 1784 publication *Flora Japonica*. Having caught sight of the plant Martin Vahl (1749-1804), Professor of Botany at Copenhagen, concluded that it wasn't a lilac and created the genus *Forsythia* in 1804. Later *F. suspensa* reached Holland in 1833 but it did not come to Britain until the 1850s.

Meanwhile, *Forsythia viridissima* arrived in Britain, from China, in a consignment of plants collected by the Scottish plant collector Robert Fortune (1812-80) and sent to the RHS in 1844. In China, the plant had been cultivated for a long time and was commonly known as 'golden bells' on account of the shape of the flower as it opened. Our narrative's focus though, *Forsythia x intermedia*, is a hybrid between *F. suspensa* and *F. viridissima*, described in 1885 by the German botanist Hermann Zabel (1832-1912) who spotted the seedlings in the Botanic Garden of Göttingen.

The genus commemorated William Forsyth (1737-1804), the superintendent of the Royal Gardens in Kensington and St James's Palace, and a founder member of the RHS. He was a gentleman who had become embroiled in a scandal, of his own making I hasten to add, concerning his alleged 'miracle cure' for dead, diseased or dying trees. His 'plaister', a patch essentially, made from cow dung, lime plaster, wood ashes and sand, even convinced the government, who were anxious to maitain good timber essential for ship building, to award him money. Forsyth died amidst the fallout before it all got completely out of hand, probably just as well.

Early in the twentieth century, *F. x intermedia* achieved a great deal of commercial success, hence its overwhelming presence in and around the suburban gardens of the new towns and commuter belts that sprang up across Britain. Each spring brings forth a blast of brilliant yellow from the leafless pimpled stems of forsythias and creates a striking sight. *Forsythia x intermedia*, the one most widely grown, is a commonplace shrub and it certainly makes its presence felt for a brief period of time.

As a cheap and cheerful plant, forsythia has been routinely specified for contractual planting in municipal spaces. One landscape architect took the idea of mass planting to a completely different level in the 1920s, Beatrix Farrand (neé Jones, 1872–1959), the only female founding member of the American Society of Landscape Architects.

At Dumbarton Oaks, the estate of philanthropists Robert Woods Bliss and wife Mildred, in Washington, DC, Farrand was commissioned to redesign the 27 acres surrounding the house. Mildred and Beatrix worked together on the garden for many years. It included a celebrated dell where the formal part of the garden ended and the informal parkland of the garden began. When we think of a dell, it is invariably a secluded hollow smothered in multi-coloured rhododendrons. Farrand decided to apply a similar single planting scheme, but using forsythias instead, in the small valley at Dumbarton Oaks.

The Forsythia Dell originally covered a whole acre and was the most dramatic area that Farrand planted, featuring only one variety of forsythia. In 1960, Mildred remarked that, 'the onrush of spring at Dumbarton Oaks fairly leaves one breathless before the great billowing mass of forsythia tumbling down two hillsides turned to gold'. There was even a 'Forsythia Gate', at the bottom of the dell, marking a formal border between the gardens and the Park.

Unusually for a designer, Farrand provided explicit instructions on the maintenance and future management of the planting at Dumbarton Oaks after the estate was acquired by Harvard University, in 1941, and the lower naturalistic areas, including the dell became a public park. In the *Plant Book for Dumbarton Oaks*, she outlines her plan for each of the gardens, stipulating they should be cared for in order to retain their basic character and integrity. Regarding the Forsythia Dell, she wrote: 'It is essential that the Forsythia be kept all alike in variety, as the intrusion of different shades of flower and different habits of shrub-growth would be unpleasant and would spoil the glory of the golden flowers ... but where a plant distinctly shows it has outlived its beauty, it should be replaced by some of the rooted runners from the hillside.'

Farrand's extensive use of the *Forsythia* species and its cultivars, especially *F. intermedia* 'Spectabilis' was said to be the backbone of many of her design initiatives. Over time, most of these have been redesigned by more contemporary gardeners; however, at Dumbarton Oaks Park the golden yellow flowers in the Forsythia Dell glow en masse for a few short weeks each spring, creating high drama, before being replaced by the lush green of foliage as if they had never been.

HEDGING YOUR BETS

Hardy fuchsia

Fuchsia magellanica 'Riccartonii'

T ravelling the south-west of Ireland, it is impossible to miss the joyous sight of the seemingly exotic hedgerows of *Fuchsia magellanica* 'Riccartonii' flowering in all their glory. Their unmistakeable blood red and deep purple pendulous flowers are reminiscent of delicate little ballerinas balancing on wire-thin stalks. These ostensibly delicate flowers belie the fierce hardiness of the plant, hence its common name, the hardy fuchsia, which has adapted so well to the Emerald Isle.

F. magellanica is actually a native of southern Chile and Argentina, near the Magellan Straits. It is known as *Chilco* by the largest group of Indigenous Peoples, the Mapuche, who have used the plant's leaves and bark to treat a variety of ailments. The berries were also consumed, being described as having a pleasant lemony taste, but in 1879, popular Victorian gardening writer James Shirley Hibberd, who could always be relied upon to tell it like it is, suggested that although they made 'very good tarts', their flavour was 'somewhat poverty stricken'.

The doughty, salt resistant *F. magellanica* 'Riccartonii' arrived on the shores of Ireland in the mid-nineteenth century and became so naturalised along the country's roads and shady lanes that it now bears the Irish name of *Deora Dé*, which translates as 'Tears of God' because of the flower's shape. *F. magellanica* 'Riccartonii' is now by far the most popular and attractive shrub for informal hedges throughout the British Isles.

The Italian sounding 'Riccartonii' is a hybrid that was raised around 1830 by James Young, gardener to Sir James Gibson-Craig at his Riccarton estate to the south of Edinburgh. Young later received a silver medal from the Caledonian Horticultural Society for it. In August 1876, James McNab of the Royal Botanic Garden Edinburgh wrote to Sir Joseph Dalton Hooker at Kew: 'The enclosed specimens of *Fuchsia Riccartonii* were taken off plants which have been growing ... these 22 or more years ... it certainly is the finest Fuchsia we have.' The Riccarton estate is now the site of Heriot-Watt University, where the plant remains a noted feature in and around the campus gardens.

FIRST OR LAST TO FLOWER?

Queen Olga's snowdrop

Galanthus reginae-olgae

'*T*he Snow-drop, winter's timid child, / awakes to life bedew'd with
tears,' are the opening lines of an ode to the snowdrop by the
eighteenth-century poet Mary Robinson (née Darby; 1757–1800).
A remarkable woman of many talents, Robinson was an actress, novelist,
dramatist and campaigner for women's rights. In April 2020, the Royal
Mail in the UK released sets of stamps celebrating the work of the Romantic
Poets, including Robinson. On her stamp are the first lines of 'Ode to the
Snowdrop', next to the image of a lovely clump of the common snowdrop,
Galanthus nivalis. This iconic flower has been forever burdened with being
a harbinger of spring. Colonies of snowdrops are often found naturalised
in many parts of the country at this time of year and, in most cases, in the
vicinity of the ruins of ancient monasteries, churchyards and other religious
establishments, relics of past pious spring traditions.

Well, there is absolutely nothing timid about the bold autumn flowering
Galanthus reginae-olgae, which can appear as early as September but
more usually October in some parts of the UK. In its haste to beat the
other snowdrops, its flowers emerge before the leaves begin to show. When
the foliage does eventually catch up, it has the distinguishing feature of a
conspicuous silvery line down the centre of the leaves. To my mind,
G. reginae-olgae heralds the coming of winter as the year fades.

G. reginae-olgae was first recorded and described in 1874 by the
Greek poet and botanist Theodoros Georgios Orphanides (1817–86),
who collected the plant on Mount Taygetus, in the Peloponnese region of
Greece. Described as temperamental, eccentric and a highly impatient
man, Orphanides engaged in lengthy correspondence with botanists and
botanical institutions all over the world, always in the hope of scrounging
specimens for his ever-increasing personal herbarium.

Conversely, he was not so forthcoming and refused to tell anyone
the location of where he had found his autumn flowering snowdrop. In
1880, Max Leichtlin (1831–1910), the German horticulturalist and expert
hybridiser of bulbous plants at his garden in Baden-Baden, approached
Orphanides looking to purchase bulbs of *G. reginae-olgae*. He came away

very disappointed and empty handed when his offer of 5 francs for a single bulb was rejected – Orphanides insisted on 50 francs each! Sadly, in February 1886, Orphanides suffered a breakdown and was hospitalised; he died five months later. The knowledge of the snowdrop's origin went to the grave with him. The plant also mysteriously disappeared from his own garden and *G. reginae-olgae* was totally lost to cultivation.

Despite Mary Robinson's early praise of the humble snowdrop, little attention had been paid to it until the early nineteenth century when poets such as William Wordsworth and Samuel Taylor Coleridge began to write about it as a romantic symbol of purity and innocence. People started to admire and take note of the flower's subtle green and white markings, and 'Galanthomania', the cult of the snowdrop, was born.

Ordinary gardeners and botanists alike paid closer attention to this small flower only to discover an infinite number of variations in shape, colour and form in each plant. People collected, selected, bred and named each exciting little gem, which could only really be appreciated at ground level on your hands and knees. This surge in interest peaked in the 1880s with new species and cultivars appearing, culminating in the 1891 RHS Snowdrop Conference. The term 'Galanthophile' was coined to describe connoisseurs and others who became devoted or obsessed collectors and admirers of snowdrops, and I proudly count myself among them.

So, can you imagine the excitement when *G. reginae-olgae* and its quirky autumnal habits were rediscovered in 1896? Even with modern breeding practices, no snowdrop blooms quite as early (or late). *Galanthus reginae-olgae* was named after the Russian-born queen of Greece, Olga Konstantinova (1851-1926), a granddaughter of Tsar Nicholas I of Russia and grandmother to the late Prince Philip, Duke of Edinburgh (1921-2021).

Historically, such unusual species and cultivars were exchanged or gifted among the snowdrop cognoscenti who could truly appreciate them. Especially at those illustrious invitation-only 'Snowdrop Luncheons', at which eagle-eyed Galanthophiles' eyes dart about in ecstasy looking for their next prized possession. Nowadays, most new or rare specimens that do come on the market command astronomical prices; Galanthomania is definitely not for the timid.

FLOWERS OF THE SEA

Stemless gentian

Gentiana acaulis

Instantly recognisable because of its startling blue colour, *Gentiana acaulis* is the epitome of the rock and alpine garden and is native to the European Alps, famous for its clean air. Therefore unsurprisingly, in 1788 *Curtis's Botanical Magazine* recorded: 'As most Alpine plants do, this loves a pure air, ... it is however somewhat capricious, ... at any rate it will not prosper near London.'

In general, it is very rare that people associate flowers with warships, merchant ships and submarines. However, in 1938, on the cusp of the Second World War, a new class of small ships was manufactured for the British Royal Navy to act as escorts for the merchant ships bringing supplies from North America to Britain, which were vulnerable to attack.

The convoy escort ships were originally named after flowers. They became known as Flower-class corvettes, *corvette* from the French for 'sloop', a name suggested by Winston Churchill, later the inspiration for Chevrolet's 1953 luxury sports car. These vessels were small, easy to manoeuvre and cheaper than other ships to construct. On 6 August 1940, HMS *Gentian* was launched in one of the first batches of the Flower-class corvettes.

Nearly 300 such vessels were built, their sole duties to escort and provide protection for convoys as part of the Battle of the Atlantic. The 'flowers' are believed to have formed the backbone of the escort fleet.

In the midst of the war, in 1941, the market town of Kington, Herefordshire, adopted HMS *Gentian* for 'Warship Week'. This was a nationwide savings campaign aimed at cities, towns and villages, and focused on raising enough funds to 'adopt' a warship. Once the target money was raised, the local community supplied the ship's crew with warm items of clothing.

HMS *Gentian* was finally scrapped on 21 August 1947, after having taken part in over sixty convoys. In the language of flowers, the gentian is said to be symbolic of justice and victory – how very apt for its namesake.

IN LOVE AND DEATH

Cherry pie

Heliotropium arborescens syn. *Heliotropium peruviana*

When *Heliotropium arborescens* was first introduced to Europe, its scent was said to be reminiscent of a freshly baked cherry pie, with a hint of vanilla and almonds, a mouthwatering description indeed. Hence its common name, cherry pie.

H. arborescens is not a showy plant. Its numerous tiny blossoms range from a pale lilac to a rich purple colour, and it is invariably located by following your nose. This is how it came to the attention of Joseph de Jussieu (1704-79) a French naturalist and physician on Charles-Marie de la Condamine's topographical expedition to Quito, Ecuador, in 1735. Jussieu was 'intoxicated with delight' when the scent drew him to a tall, unprepossessing shrub in a valley while on his way south from Quito to Lima, Peru.

He named the plant heliotrope, from the Greek *helios* for sun and *tropos* to turn, as he had observed that all the small florets appeared to be facing the sun. He then dispatched seeds to the royal gardens in Paris, where, in 1740, the plant flowered before being distributed to the rest of Europe. *H. arborescens* arrived in Britain in 1757 when Philip Miller at the Chelsea Physic Garden, in London, received seeds from the Duke d'Ayen's botanic garden at Saint-Germain-en-Laye, France.

Joseph Jussieu collected a good deal of plants over a long period of time and eventually returned to France in 1771 after an absence of thirty-six years. The heliotrope was, indeed, a wonderful introduction to the country; however, that was not all that Jussieu collected and sent to the Jardin du Roi. He was the first explorer to collect botanical specimens of *Erythroxylum coca* - or using its more common name, cocaine. The juxtaposition of these two introductions is truly extraordinary.

H. arborescens has long been a votive flower, especially in its native country where it was offered in fulfilment of a vow and in matters of the heart. The acceptance of heliotrope flowers by a woman from her beau was considered to be a mutual acceptance of an engagement. Naturally, the heliotrope became known as *herbe d'amour*, or the flower of love, with cultivars bearing flirtatious names such as 'beauty of the boudoir'.

Despite being associated with love, it was also closely linked with mourning. During the Victorian era, etiquette was everything, especially for women. Following the loss of her husband, a widow wore specific mourning attire deemed acceptable to society. The mourning period could last up to two and a half years and encompassed different stages. The first, 'full' mourning, required matt, never shiny, black fabric such as crepe. Then came the stage when a widow could wear subdued 'secondary mourning colours', like mauve and lilac. And so, inevitably, the mauvish purple shade of *H. arborescens* was immortalised as a colour in its own right. 'Heliotrope' was added to the palette of suitable colours for the last stages of mourning. Predictably, in the language of flowers, heliotrope came to symbolise devotion or attachment. It became so popular it even emerged in the arts of the day – in Oscar Wilde's 1895 play, *An Ideal Husband*, the antagonistic Mrs Cheveley enters a party, with all eyes on her, 'in heliotrope, with diamonds'.

As the century progressed, the abundance of affordable glasshouses helped to popularise the plant, which could now be overwintered as rooted cuttings, and used in the increasing trend of 'bedding out' for summer displays. *H. arborescens* filled the high Victorian gardens' parterres with intricate designs not only to please the eye but also the senses.

The popularity of heliotropes reached their peak in the early 1920s, when the country house tradition attempted to recreate the bygone opulence of the belle époque of the Edwardian era when they seemed to be everywhere. Even the popular but often waspish garden writer James Shirley Hibberd had conceded that, 'the heliotrope is an interesting beauty, and one of the most desirable plants wherewith to perfume a conservatory or a garden, or to fill a button-hole'.

DISH OF THE DAY

Daylily

Hemerocallis fulva

The genus *Hemerocallis* means 'beauty for the day', and there is something very satisfying about wondering round a flower border plucking the faded blooms of a daylily, knowing that come the morning more flowers will appear to take their place.

Daylilies were known to the early Roman, Greek and Egyptian doctors from plants brought from China along the silk routes about 2,000 years ago. Northern Europe only learned of them in the sixteenth century, with *Hemerocallis fulva* introduced in 1576. By 1597, Gerard), who coined the English term 'daylily', recorded: 'These lilies do grow in my garden, as also in the gardens of herbarists, and lovers of fine and rare plants; but not wild in England as in other countries.' Fast forward several hundred years and many Americans would probably disagree with the 'rarity' sentiment since *H. fulva*, a natural coloniser given half a chance, has become so naturalised in many rural parts of the country, verily galloping along the roadside and in ditches, earning itself the rather unflattering common name of ditch lily.

As early as 1812, alarm bells might have already started ringing about the potentially invasive nature of the flower, when Anglo-American botanist Thomas Nuttall (see page 189) observed in his publication, *The Genera of North American Plants,* how *H. fulva* had naturalised in moist meadows around Philadelphia and along parts of the banks of the Schuylkill River. This, incidentally, was the location of botanist John Bartram's (1699-1777) garden, who founded the oldest surviving botanic garden in the United States. In 1728, *H. fulva* appeared in his plant lists. Nuttall concluded that he would mark *H. fulva's* future progress, and noted that it was 'as easily to impose upon a stranger for an indigenous plant'. How prophetic these words were.

According to the Chinese botanist and academic Hui-lin Li (1911-2002), in his 1959 publication *The Garden Flowers of China,* the original home of *H. fulva* has never really been determined, since the plant has not been collected in the wild. Li suggested that the plant may have originated as a chance seedling hundreds of years ago that was brought into cultivation. He also recorded that it was possible that 'all plants that have been in cultivation throughout several centuries and still in cultivation were derived from this one seedling'.

This is entirely possible because the cultivated plant is a triploid with three, instead of two, sets of chromosomes and is usually infertile, rarely sets seeds and its invasive nature is due to its fleshy spreading roots, which like the rest of the plant are edible as well as the source of a variety of remedies for diverse human ailments. In ancient China, *H. fulva* was known as the 'sorrow-free herb', as it was believed the blossoms, if eaten, had the power to alleviate sorrow.

Unbeknown to the everyday gardener, the daylily can be a veritable culinary and medicinal wonder but as ever, once displaced from its native habitat, it became a mere garden ornament to be admired purely for its beauty. Therefore, as *H. fulva* marched through various parts of the western world seeking adoration for its looks and new habitats to colonise, over in the Far East, people were munching their way through the plant, where it was grown for its consumption and medicinal values rather than its ornamental display. Of particular gastronomic interest and delight are the plant's flower buds, known as '*gum jum choi*' (dried lily buds) or 'golden needles' in China.

The flower buds are picked very early in the morning, just at the point before they fully open, in order to preserve the aroma and flavour. Once collected, they are steamed and spread on mats to dry in the sun. The dried buds have to be rehydrated before being added to recipes and generally have a golden-caramel colour and earthy flavour and texture. Therefore, dried lily buds provide an inexpensive but nutritious and abundant ingredient.

In some areas of East Asia, *H. fulva* is grown as a vegetable on an industrial scale, with numerous fields covering hundreds of acres. Some of these daylily fields are now left unharvested to form the most picturesque views of the flowers in all their glory across the countryside. These have become an extremely popular tourist destination between August to September, when local restaurants and food stands serve visitors deep fried snacks and other dishes made with the daylily buds and flower stems. The cultivation of the daylily in this manner is a classic example of what flowers can mean to different communities. As with many of the plants that we grow in our own gardens and delight in, the majority of them would originally have been grown in their home country purely for practical purposes, and if they also happen to be beautiful then so much the better.

John Gerard
(1545–1612)

Gerard's 1597 publication, *Herball, or generall historie of plantes,* was one of the earliest herbals written in English, describing over 200 plants, along with their qualities, cultural requirements and uses. A good deal of the text had been largely derived from another herbal of 1554 by the Flemish physician and botanist Rembert Dodoens, and many of the illustrations already published. Gerard, an avid collector of plants, had his own garden at Holborn, London, where he cultivated hundreds of 'rare and fine' specimens, including the newly arrived potato. In 1596, he compiled a catalogue of the plants in his garden, which included the first reference to many of the introduced and indigenous plants we now grow in our gardens. The man's enthusiasm and sometimes exaggerated responses to the characteristics of certain plants is extremely endearing at times. Gerard's *Herball* was revised in 1633 into a more scholarly edition by Thomas Johnson who amended some inaccuracies while adding 800 new plants and many more illustrations.

GOFFERED FRILLS AND CUFFS

English bluebell

Hyacinthoides non-scripta

W ho can resist the glorious sight of bluebells en masse nestling under the dappled shade of an ancient woodland canopy? Over half of the world's bluebell population grows in the UK. As a native flower, the bluebell is an important indicator species when identifying ancient woodlands, since these environments have quietly evolved over hundreds of years. But for a few short weeks each year, in late spring, these woods become a delicate sea of blue signalling a seasonal milestone.

In his 1597 *Herball,* Gerard called the bluebell *Hyacinthus anglicus,* or the English Hyacinth, because it grew so abundantly in England. Unlike other woodland plants such as the primrose, which were brought into gardens at an early stage for their medicinal properties, the bluebell's toxicity ensured that it remained relatively undisturbed to flourish in the woods.

Gerard wrote that the bluebell's 'root is bulbous, full of a slimy gluish juice … whereof is made the best starch next unto that of Wake-robin roots'. Wake-robin or starchwort referred to another woodland plant, *Arum maculatum,* which was said to produce a purer and whiter form of starch.

Although the starching of fine fabrics, lace and laundry was already in practice in Britain, an increase in the knowledge of its use came with the arrival of migrants from France in the 1560s. One particular woman, a skilled Flemish ruff maker called Mistress Dingham van der Plasse arrived in London and promptly set up in business. The 'Dutch Lady' charged up to £5 for lessons and ladies of the house, local seamstresses and household servants flocked to learn the art of starching and setting ruffs. Her arrival coincided with the escalating and utterly impractical fashion for wearing neck ruffs and cuffs, enjoyed by a certain class of men, women and children from the mid-sixteenth century into the seventeenth century.

The ruff was also known as a goffered frill, which referred to a length of linen or cotton being pressed into pleats with heated irons. However, when they were starched, they could be more elaborate and size became equated to power: put simply, the bigger one's ruff the greater one's wealth

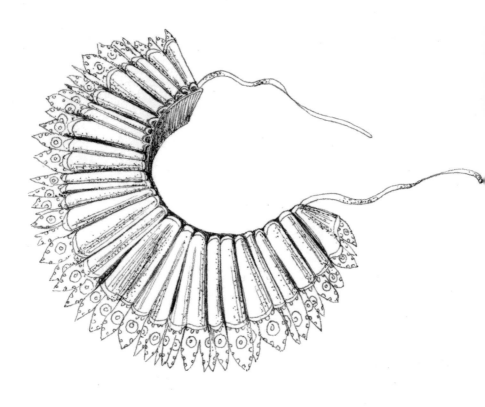

and social status. In the absence of other sources of starch, demand rose for bluebell bulbs because, when crushed, their gluey extract provided a starch substitute for these much sought after goffered frills.

For every admirer of a trend there is always a critic, however, and as far as the ruff was concerned, the notoriously devout Puritan and activist Mr Phillip Stubbes (c. 1555–1610), took an exception to them. In 1583, he wrote extensively about the evils of ruffs and those who wore them, denouncing them as 'great and monstrous' made with 'liquide matter they call starch', which he roundly condemned as being the devil's liquor. Who would have thought that bluebell bulb starch could arouse such passion?

Like so many plants that have been around a long time, the bluebell has endured many name changes, often instigated by whoever regarded themselves as the authority at that particular time. According to John Parkinson, the Flemish botanist and physician Rembert Dodoens (1517–85) initially called the English bluebell *Hyacinthoides non scriptus*, which literally translates as the 'unwritten-on hyacinth-like plant'. *Non scriptus* means 'unlettered' or 'unmarked', to distinguish it from the mythical hyacinth flower which was said to have been marked by the god Apollo's tears of lament over the death of his lover, Hyacinthus. But Parkinson qualified that the reason Dodoens chose the name was because 'it was not written of by any author before himselfe'. The name that Linnaeus used in his 1753 publication, *Species plantarum*, was *Hyacinthoides non-scripta*.

Regardless of the whys and wherefores, the *non-scripta* irritated the president of the Linnaean Society, James Edward Smith (1759–1828) who, in 1797, remarked that anything would be better as it didn't do the plant justice. *Scilla nutans* was Smith's solution, *nutans* meaning 'nodding' or 'drooping' – describing the flower's bashful appearance so well. This is perhaps why, in that much loved Victorian language of flowers, the bluebell's demeanour represents humility, as well as being a symbol of constancy, presumably because of its longevity within our ancient forests.

The word bluebell as a common name only emerged in the early nineteenth century, when Romantic poets like John Clare (1793–1864), took their inspiration from the countryside and wrote about gathering bluebell flowers. Another poet, Gerard Manley Hopkins (1844–89), was particularly enthralled with the bluebell and has been credited with being the first person to observe and document that within a woodland the bluebells would be 'all hanging their heads one way'. The reason for this is unclear but during a walk in an ancient woodland, you may notice that they all tend to bend to the south. Perhaps they are in search of the time-limited light through the early leaf canopy before full shade returns.

ILLUMINATORS AND MINIATURISTS UNITE IN GREEN

Bearded iris

Iris germanica

The genus *Iris*, with its infinite variation of colour, was aptly named after the Greek goddess Iris, the personification of the rainbow. Throughout the centuries, different iris flowers have yielded colourants ranging from yellows and greens through to blues and greys. In *De coloribus et artibus Romanorum (On the colours and arts of the Romans)*, the medieval historian Eraclius observed: 'He who wishes to convert flowers into the various colours which, for the purpose of writing, the page of a book demands, must wander over the cornfields early in the morning, and then he will find various flowers fresh sprung up.'

Iris germanica, with its deep purple-blue flower petals, is said to be an ancient natural hybrid, introduced to Britain by the Romans during their occupation from AD 43. When they subsequently withdrew from the country 400 years later, following the fall of the Roman Empire, *I. germanica* was well established, continuing to thrive well into the Middle Ages, usually enclosed in the security of monastic gardens. Here, the monks devoted a great deal of time to their plants, which were central to the production of food as well as for flowers and herbs crucial for medicinal and other utilitarian purposes.

The monks, in their little scriptoria, were also the sole makers of highly ornate, illuminated manuscripts – the ultimate organic product – all created from a variety of natural resources including parchment, which was made from animal skins. The parchment borders were elaborately decorated with quirky miniature paintings and grotesque hybrid creatures, often highly amusing and alarming in equal measure. These drolleries or little thumbnail paintings were embellished with gold and silver leaf that 'illuminated' the text and illustrations reflecting the light. A range of organic pigments were used to colour the letters and images, including iris green, derived from *Iris germanica*, which was grown widely in monastic gardens.

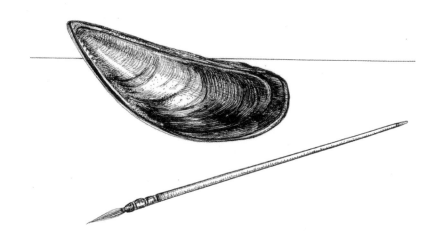

The seasonal production of iris green involved gathering the petals of the flower, which were then pounded in order to release the juice. Small, dry linen squares or 'clothlets', which had been pre-treated with a mordant or fixative, were then dipped in the purple juice. The clothlets were left to dry before being rewetted in the juice; the whole process was repeated up to ten times until all the juice was absorbed into a collection of 'stained' clothlets used as a reservoir to store the colour. These clothlets were dried and secured in between the pages of a book until such time as the colour was needed by the illuminator. To release the colour, the clothlet was placed in a dish and moistened with glair or egg white, which became a clear, bright green when this was added. The colour was then squeezed into little pots ready to use. The monks had access to a wide range of plant material in order to produce other pigments such as sap green derived from the berries of buckthorn (*Rhamnus*), the main rival of iris green.

Inevitably, the production of illuminated manuscripts gradually disappeared with the invention of the European printing press in the second half of the fifteenth century, as illumination was replaced with printed illustrations. Nevertheless, iris green found a new calling when it became a highly prized commodity by the painters of miniature portraits of the late sixteenth and early seventeenth centuries. This genre of art emerged from techniques used in the illuminated manuscript tradition.

These miniaturist painters were also known as 'limners' from the term 'limning', derived from the Latin *luminare*, meaning 'to give light' or illuminate. Limners used squirrel hair brushes and mixed their colours and binder in a mussel shell, which made for a perfect miniature palette. In the days before photography, these small paintings, which could be held in the palm of your hand, usually depicted a lover, a family member or a close friend and were highly prized.

In 1803, *Curtis's Botanical Magazine* confirmed that a pigment, 'chiefly used by miniature painters, called *verdelis*, *Vert d'iris* or *iris-green* is made from its [*Iris germanica's*] flowers'.

There were plenty of instructions available for making colours from iris petals, and even as late as 1829, *Iris germanica* was still used to produce paint for artists, as Henry Phillips cheerfully noted: 'The common blue or purple of our gardens, *Iris germanica*, yields a most beautiful paint for water-colours.' Now, I have been known to dabble once in a while with watercolours and the idea of painting with a pigment that I have created from scratch sounds absolutely marvellous. However, the gardener in me recoils at the thought of removing those gorgeous petals and destroying my beautiful iris border; therefore I will leave the dedicated artist to do what they will.

FLOWER CROWNS FOR THE MASSES

Common jasmine

Jasminum officinale

O f all the senses, smell is, for many people, most closely associated with memory, always guaranteed to bring back a wealth of nostalgic moments. *Jasminum officinale* has been cultivated for its scent for so long, in many countries, it's impossible to say with any certainty its country of origin. However, from the fourth century, Chinese authors recorded it as an 'exotic' plant, suggesting that it came from Persia, now modern-day Iran. Its beautiful fragrance and versatility ensured its swift addition to China's already bountiful botanical treasures.

Historically, the Pearl River Delta in the Kwangtung, now Guangdong Province, was one of the most fertile areas in southern China. Jasmine gardens, cultivated mainly for the flower buds, proliferated for miles along the banks of the river. A seventeenth-century account, *Notes on Kwangtung Province*, described how, just before dawn, women collected thousands of unopened jasmine buds, which would later open at dusk when the scent was at its strongest.

The buds were wrapped in wet cloth before the flower merchants crossed the river to buy them to sell in the city, where they were strung together by hundreds of workers to create decorative objects, such as flower crowns. The distinguished scholar Li T'iao-yüan (1734–1803) wrote, in 1777, that, '[a]fter these fragrant buds are placed on the head, they begin to open ... they become more fragrant with human warmth, lasting the whole night and lingering until dawn'.

Garlands of flower buds were routinely used to decorate buildings and the eaves of houseboats during religious ceremonies. The quantities of buds required daily for such display must have been immense, as the flowers were also used to flavour food and wine, and to perfume tea.

The scent of jasmine has always been closely associated with romance: no assignation was complete without a moment or two beneath a jasmine-festooned arbour. Gerard, growing it in England in 1597, described how 'claspeth ... about such things as stand next unto it'. He heartily endorsed planting jasmine against banqueting houses. One can only imagine the clasping that went on in those secluded romantic garden buildings ...

IMPRESSIONS OF NATURE

Red hot poker

Kniphofia uvaria syn. *Aloe uvaria* and *Tritoma uvaria*

When, in 1753, Linnaeus bestowed the name *Aloe uvaria* on a peculiar looking plant introduced into Europe from the Cape of Good Hope around 1700, he did so because its inflorescence before opening reminded him of a tiny bunch of grapes (*uva* being Latin for 'grape'). But in 1794, the German botanist Conrad Moench moved the plant into the genus *Kniphofia*, which he had especially created in honour of the German physician Johannes Hieronymus Kniphof (1704-63).

This new generic name, however, was not really taken up until around 1843, when the nomenclature was reviewed. In the meantime, in 1804, John Bellenden Ker Gawler (1764-1842), botanist, *bon viveur* and man of fashion, decided to assign the plant to the genus *Tritoma*, resulting in *Tritoma uvaria*. Even though *Kniphofia* had been in general use in scientific literature for years, the name *Tritoma* became so widely used in Britain and America that it can still be seen in nursery catalogues even today. In fariness, I suspect the reason *Tritoma* remained more popular was because it was far easier to spell and pronounce.

Between 1757 and 1764, Kniphof, a very keen botanist, produced one of his best-known works, *Botanica in Originali*. It was a ground-breaking publication with 1,200 botanical illustrations produced by Kniphof himself using the method of nature printing.

This technique, involving taking an impression directly from plants or other natural objects to create an image on paper, has been around for centuries. It was practised by Leonardo da Vinci (1452-1519).

One of the earliest surviving nature prints, from around 1508, is of a *Salvia officinalis* or sage leaf in the *Codex Atlanticus*, a 12-volume set of drawings and writings by da Vinci. The artist used the ancient method of blackening the leaf over the smoke of an oil lamp before pressing it between sheets of paper. The sooty pigment, known as lamp-black, defined the outline of the leaf, transferring it to the paper. In his *Codex*, da Vinci described in detail how to make nature prints from plants.

The increased popularity of herbals in Europe in the sixteenth century helped to popularise nature printing, and by using da Vinci's basic method of inking plant specimens, botanists and artists alike created unique prints which were better than some of the existing woodcuts of medicinal plants. It was a convenient and accurate way of recording useful plants.

Aloe uvaria, as it was then known, had the honour of being included in Kniphof's unique publication, the image dated 1762. Once again, da Vinci's method was used but this time with a new twist: Kniphof transformed the technique by colouring in the black and white plant impressions by hand. Prior to this, all the nature print impressions had been solely black on white.

As a botanist himself, Kniphof saw the value of nature printing in the growing science of botany and for the recording and identification of plants. This method had a huge advantage, as it did not require a skilled botanical artist or expensive equipment, but it was incredibly laborious. These nature prints resembled flattened herbarium specimens and had some advantages over herbaria because the preserved plant specimens were susceptible to insect damage and often became fragile.

By the late eighteenth and early nineteenth centuries, many more renowned botanists were using nature printing in their plant-collecting activities. The German polymath Alexander von Humbolt (1769-1859) created a set of nature prints during his travels in the Americas, an insurance against the loss of any dried plant samples collected – every collector's worst nightmare, losing months' (and in some cases years') worth of specimens.

Over the years I have come to the conclusion that you either love or hate red hot pokers, but due to their permanently tatty-looking leaves I remain undecided. Dear old James Shirley Hibberd, never one to mince his words, was definitely in the latter camp when he complained about the lack of species – 'the few there are, are more than are wanted from the gardener's point of view', but, he sniffed, if gardeners must plant them, then they needed 'a little extra care to avoid a violation of good taste'.

Having said that, the ubiquitous hot border arguably would be much poorer without the inclusion of those searing red hot pokers.

James Shirley Hibberd
(1825–90)

Hibberd was a suburban gardener, prolific best-selling horticultural writer and journalist who brought amateur gardening to the masses. He was also an advocate and trailblazer for urban gardening. His first book in 1855, *Town Gardens: A Manual for the Management of City and Suburban Gardens*, was followed by *Rustic Adornments for Homes of Taste*, in 1856. Writing from personal experience, he focused on innovative horticultural methods, new plants, advice on decorating the home, designing town gardens and the pleasures of urban beekeeping. His obituary in 1890 in *The Gardeners' Chronicle* stated: 'It is, we fear but too probable that he fell a victim of his own zeal.' Certainly, one of his greatest achievements was founding the *Amateur Gardener Magazine* in 1884. Sadly the final edition, after 139 years, was published on 14 October 2023.

EMBROIDERED HEARTS

Bleeding heart

Lamprocapnos spectabilis syn. *Dicentra spectabilis*

Lamprocapnos spectabilis, more commonly known as 'bleeding heart', is a native of China, where it has long been cultivated as *Ho Pao mou dan* or purse moutan, because its leaves resemble those of the tree peony. '*Mou dan*' is one of several Chinese names for tree peonies and means 'most beautiful'.

The 'purse moutan' is rooted in an ancient love story that tells of a beautiful and honourable woman who continually rejected suitors seemingly without reason. After a time, it was discovered that she already had a secret love who had joined the army and would be away for two years without any means of communicating with her. So, she vowed to wait patiently for his return. Each month, she delicately embroidered a little purse decorated with flowers for her absent love, hanging them on the branches of a tree peony which grew by her window. In time, the plant was covered in these little heart-shaped purses. As a reward for the woman's patience and devotion, the gods transformed her tree peony along with all its small purses into a living plant, hence the resemblance in its foliage.

In 1742, the French Jesuit missionary and amateur botanist Pierre le Chéron d'Incarville (1706-57) sent seeds of bleeding heart from Beijing to his mentor, Bernard de Jussieu, director of the Jardin du Roi in Paris. *L. spectabilis* subsequently popped up in Britain around 1810, only to just as swiftly disappear.

It was over thirty years before it was seen again in Britain, when China became more accessible to Europeans and the Scottish botanist Robert Fortune (1813-80) acquired the plant from the garden of a Chinese official on the island of Zhoushan. It was reintroduced in 1846 and the Victorians adored it so much that it soon found its way into the parlour, where the distinctive flowers were reproduced on textiles and wallpapers.

In his 1883 publication, *The English Flower Garden*, William Robinson remarked how popular the plant had become and delighted in the singular flowers which he said were 'suspended in strings and resemble rosy hearts'. Of course, those 'rosy hearts' greatly appealed to the romantic Victorians who promptly adopted *L. spectabilis* as a symbol of fidelity and undying love.

GROWTH IN ADVERSITY

Sweet pea

Lathyrus odoratus

The idyllic summer that has become so ingrained in British society is usually signalled by the multicoloured and deliciously scented arrangements of sweet peas upon gingham tablecloths, surrounded by an array of crustless sandwiches. But these big, often frilled and billowy sweet peas, while gorgeous, are a far cry from the delicate sweetly scented deep blue and purple species of *Lathyrus odoratus*. The Sicilian Father Francesco Cupani (1657-1710), a provincial botanist, came across the plant and later described it in his *Hortus Catholicus Neapolitanus* of 1696. Father Cupani shared his collected seeds with friends, in particular the Dutch botanist, Dr Caspar Commelin in Amsterdam. He noted that the 'butterfly like flowers ... are large and have a purple standard, the remaining petals are sky-blue. These flowers have a very pleasant smell.'

From Cupani's wider botanical network, the plant, which was greatly admired, spread rapidly until it came on the commercial market in 1724 as 'sweet sented pease'. But it took many more years, to the 1800s, for breeders to cast an eye over the sweet pea and note its potential profitability. Very soon, a wide-ranging palette of colours began to emerge. As the century marched on, the sweet pea was subjected to all sorts of crossing and back-crossing, to produce a kaleidoscope of colours and markings – often at the cost of its characteristic perfume.

The demand for it spread across the Atlantic and from 1897, American nurserymen like W. Attlee Burpee were producing new varieties that could withstand the hotter summer climate and be commercially produced for the cut flower industry.

Meanwhile, the first Japanese immigrants began to arrive in America from the late 1860s. By 1905, some of them had gravitated towards Arizona, intent on farming mainly vegetables. In the 1930s, the Nakagawa family had decided to farm at the base of the South Mountains of Phoenix. Just as their hard work was beginning to pay off, the Second World War crashed into America with the attack on Pearl Harbour. Japanese–Americans were then targeted and forced to sell or give up their land and move into internment camps. The Nakagawas and others were incarcerated in a centre south-east of

Phoenix for the duration of the war. When they were finally released in 1945, they found their livelihoods had been destroyed.

The Nakagawas, along with six other Japanese–American families, the Kishiyamas, Maruyamas, Nakamuras, Sakatos, Iwakoshis and Watanabes, began establishing new farms all over again. Although the land required back-breaking labour to remove the rocks and stones by hand, as well as creating an irrigation system, the protection at the base of the mountain created an advantageous microclimate. Through hard work and sheer determination, by the 1950s, they had re-established thriving flower and vegetable farms.

For the next thirty years the Nakagawa's flower farm, situated along Baseline Road, South Phoenix thrived. They grew an array of flowers, including scented stocks and sweet peas. In order to get high-quality sweet peas for cutting, they grew them on cordons or single flower stems, trained on supports with very short side-shoots. This resulted in larger flowers on

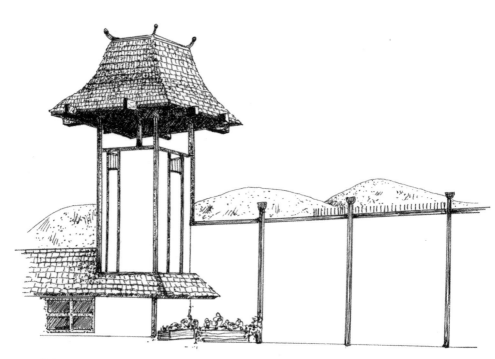

very long stems. In early summer, visitors travelled across states to buy bouquets from the flower stands or just to drive past the fields. The scent was said to carry for miles and drivers would roll down their windows to make the most of the beautiful scent as they drove by mile after mile.

Throughout the 1960s and 1970s, the Phoenix Japanese flower families and their colourful fields were a tourist destination, inspiring them to harness this increased attention. So, in 1969, Nick Hiroshi Nakagawa (1923-2021) built a three-storey pagoda tower with a viewing platform; this gave the visitors a stunning view of what must have looked like a giant tapestry of flowers.

The flower farm shipped boxes of flowers across the nation, and the tin sheds which had been used to sell vegetables and flowers from now became proper shops. The Nakagawa's was called Baseline Flower Growers.

Slowly over the years the other Japanese-American flower farmers gradually sold off their land to developers. Today, all the flower fields on Baseline Road have long gone. The last remaining flower shop is Baseline Flower Growers, which now only sells a range of imported flowers from California and South America; it is a solitary reminder of an astonishing legacy, a time when hundreds of acres of flower fields made the brown Arizona desert bloom. The Nakagawas created a colourful oasis; there are postcards of their flower fields, including ones showing row upon row of cordons wrapped in rainbow-coloured sweet peas.

Nick Nakagawa's daughter, Kathy, an associate professor at Arizona State University, remarked that now and then someone will come to her family's shop to 'share a memory of the gardens and the farmers who turned rocks and dirt into a destination spot. In Japanese, we call this feeling *natsukashi*, "sweet memories"'; this is perhaps fitting when remembering Father Cupani's sweet and humble *Lathyrus odoratus*.

APPROPRIATION OF THE PRIMROSE SELLER

English lavender

Lavandula angustifolia

The aromatic flowers of *Lavandula angustifolia*, with their soothing and restorative qualities, are native to the Mediterranean regions, as well as some areas in northern Africa. In the sixteenth century, John Gerard enthused about its abilities to calm the 'panting and passion of the heart', although whether this applied to a medically induced condition or one of a romantic nature is hard to say.

The herb has been used for a wide range of purposes throughout many cultures for hundreds of years. During the Renaissance and Medieval periods across Europe, lavender was used for washing linen, which was then dried over lavender bushes further infusing it with its calming scent. Thus, the hired washerwomen were called *les lavandières* in France and in Italy as *la lavandaie*. Even in the seventeenth century in England the gardener and author Leonard Meager (c.1624–c.1704), suggested growing a compact lavender hedge 'to lay small cloaths upon to white [bleach] and dry'. While it is frequently suggested that the Latin *lavare*, to wash, was the source of the word, according to some botanists, as well as a 2004 monograph on the genus *Lavandula*, the name relates to the Latin *livare* 'to be livid or bluish', probably in reference to the flower's colour.

Lavender became so common that in his 1652 *The English Physitian*, later entitled *The Complete Herbal*, botanist Nicholas Culpeper (1616–54) declared that: 'Being an inhabitant almost in every garden, it is so well known, that it needs no description.'

Like many other aromatic plants lavender was routinely used for strewing upon the floor in order to combat any unpleasant odours, and in drawers to act as an insect repellent. In fact, for centuries there was even a position for a herb-strewer to royalty, which was reserved for a woman of high social standing within the court.

Certainly, lavender has always been highly valued for its cleansing and refreshing properties, and the demand for its essential oils for perfumery reached its peak in popularity during the Victorian era. When Queen

Victoria declared her love of lavender, it incited a cult-like reaction which drove the fashion for all-things lavender, leading to the rapid growth of the English lavender industry.

Back in 1770, the Cleaver family founded Yardley, now Yardley London. As purveyors of fine soaps and perfumes they were at the forefront of an industry going from strength to strength, and even had a stand at the 1851 Great Exhibition. By 1873, as their range of products increased, the company launched its signature scent of English Lavender – which was essentially lavender water. Over 300 acres of lavender were grown in and around the Surrey area to supply their expanding market.

As part of a new advertising strategy in the early twentieth century, Yardley immortalised one of a series of fourteen paintings by the English painter Francis Wheatley (1747-1801). Known as the 'Cries of London', they were created around 1791 and featured a variety of itinerant street vendors plying their trade in verse on the streets of London.

At the end of July, lavender sellers would cry, 'Come buy, my blooming lavender, sixteen branches for a penny ... buy it once, buy it twice, it makes your clothes smell very nice.' Wheatly, however, did not paint a lavender seller, although his painting of a primrose seller and her two children carrying baskets of yellow primroses caught the eye and imagination of Yardley's advertising campaigners. The image was adopted for their new corporate logo but the primroses were replaced with bundles of lavender. This new image became synonymous with Yardley London, which used it to promote its famous Old English Lavender perfume, soap and talcum powder. There is even a figurine of this lavender seller by Royal Doulton, which has become iconic and very collectable.

In 1932, Yardley sent its chief chemist John H. Seager overseas to source different species of lavender. Seager spent time in America in the company of a leading authority on lavender growing, Luther J. Wyckoff, at his farm Chambers Prairie, Washington. Wyckoff had spent the past twenty-five years trialling different lavender species, and *angustifolia* consistently produced the best oil. Seager was quite taken with the specimens he saw and took samples to study and develop back in England. On a subsequent visit, Seager arranged for 5,000 of Wyckoff's lavender cuttings to be shipped back to Yardley and Co's lavender farm, from which they developed their very own cultivar of *Lavandula angustifolia*. This species is still used in Yardley's fragrances today.

THE CARDINAL'S STOCKINGS

Cardinal flower

Lobelia cardinalis

The brilliant scarlet-flowered *Lobelia cardinalis* was first recorded by French explorers in Canada, which had been a colony of France since 1535. The first specimens were sent to France around 1621.

An illustration and description of the plant appeared in Pierre Vallet's 1623 edition of *Le Jardin du roy très chrestien Loys XIII* (*The Garden of the Most Christian King Louis XIII*). It was a most lavish *florilegium*, or collection of engravings, first published in 1608, but this new edition had a further twenty plates added to include the latest new plants. Vallet's publication was dedicated to Marie de' Medici (1575-1642), Queen Consort to Henry IV, and was intended as a botanically accurate floral pattern book for painters, embroiderers and tapestry weavers. The plants depicted were drawn from those growing in the gardens of Jean Robin (1550-1629), director of the royal gardens. Robin had originally named the plant *Trachelium Americanum flore rubro, seu planta Cardinalis* – you can see why Linnaeus' binomial or two-part naming system was welcomed with a sigh of relief 130 years later.

Robin, who was often first to receive and propagate new plants from French expeditions, travelled to London and visited John Gerard and John Tradescant the Elder (c. 1570-1638), and through Robin *Lobelia cardinalis* was introduced to Britain sometime between 1626 and 1629.

Tradescant was appointed gardener at Oatlands Palace, Surrey to the French-born Queen Henrietta Maria (1609-69), daughter of Marie de' Medici. In 1631, she wrote to her mother: 'As I am sending this man into France to get some fruit-trees and flowers, I most humbly entreat your majesty to be pleased to assist him with your power.' It is highly likely that she was referring to Tradescant. Henrietta Maria was already familiar with *L. cardinalis*, according to an 1845 publication, *The Topic*, who recorded that the name 'cardinal flower' was given to the plant by the young princess. It seems that when it was presented to her in full flower, she declared that she would have admired it 'exceedingly, if its colour had not put her so much in mind of the red stockings of Cardinal Richelieu, whom she could not endure'. Henrietta Maria was referring to the scarlet formal garments or

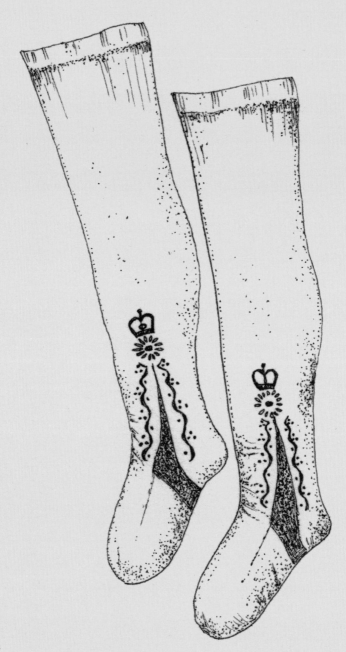

vestments worn by cardinals of the Roman Catholic Church in which she had been raised. Richelieu had for many years been her mother's ally until they fell out. As *The Topic* concludes, 'From which merrie jest of her Grace, this flower received its name.'

In 1629, John Parkinson produced his magnum opus *Paradisi in Sole Paradisus Terrestris*, which he dedicated to Queen Henrietta Maria. It was the first important English treatise on horticulture, which detailed the plants of a pleasure garden together with gardening practices and styles of the day including references to contemporary botanists and gardeners.

Parkinson wrote of how he had received a shipment of seeds of *L. cardinalis* where it 'groweth neere the river in Canada, where the French plantation in America is seated'. He described the ensuing plant as being 'a brave plant', presumably because of the intensity of its colour. The rather overly complicated name of *Trachelium Americanum flore rubro, seu planta Cardinalis* led Parkinson to give the plant the English name of 'the rich crimson Cardinal's flower.'

The plant's distinctive flowers ensured that it remained an extremely popular plant throughout the eighteenth and nineteenth centuries, with many commentators extolling its virtues. In 1754, the Scottish horticulturalist and botanist James Justice (1698-1763) was so delighted with his plant that he recommended it as 'a flower of most handsome appearance, which should not be wanting in curious gardens as it excels all other flowers in the richness of its colour'.

With such glowing comments about an historic plant, imagine how our twenty-first century plants would be received by the likes of Gerard, Parkinson, Justice and others. One thing is for sure, they would all be clamouring to get their hands on a relatively new cultivar from America, *Lobelia cardinalis* 'Chocolate Truffle' (syn. 'Black Truffle') – found growing among *L. cardinalis* seedlings a few years ago. This plant has the most divine spires of vermilion flowers above almost black, dark chocolate coloured foliage. Henrietta Maria would have loved it.

THE SURVIVAL OF THE FITTEST

Russell lupins

Lupinus 'Russell hybrids'

According to the English author and garden designer Vita Sackville-West (see page 119), there have always been sensations at the annual Chelsea Flower Show. In 1939, she recalled how 'we first saw the Russell lupins in their extraordinary variety of colour, so far removed from the old familiar blue as to seem almost a different flower'. This sensation was the result of the single-minded quest of a gentleman named George Russell (1857-1951).

Back in 1911, at the age of fifty-four, Russell had worked as a freelance gardener in York. He lived in a small, terraced house without a garden, but he had an allotment where he grew his fruit and vegetables, and where he also dabbled in the hybridisation of aquilegias, an old cottage garden favourite with a wide range of colours.

One day he noticed a vase of lupins at one of his client's houses. In all likelihood, these would have been the bluish to reddish–purple and off-white colours of the common perennial garden lupin of the time. The sight of these rather muted and dullish flowers obviously struck a chord with Russell, who with a practised eye was aware of the flower's potential.

Determined to try his luck in improving the lupin, he set about acquiring the seeds of as many plants as he could. As the seedlings emerged and flowered, Russell applied a meticulous selection and reselection regime to find the most desirable plants. Year on year, the process was repeated with a critical eye, as he ruthlessly discarded any seedling that did not meet his criteria. Russell made no notes: everything was done by sight, truly a case of survival of the fittest.

Unlike other hybridisers Russell never interfered with the natural cross-pollination process: he let nature take its course with bumblebees taking centre stage, as they have the weight to push down the 'keel' of the flower when they land to collect nectar and in turn the pollen.

Very soon, the lupins outgrew his allotment, so Russell took on a second. Over a twenty-three year period, Russell began to see sturdier and more compact spires of flowers, in a range of new and exciting colours, slowly begin to emerge.

In all the years of growing and improving his lupins, Russell steadfastly refused to sell any seeds or plants, leaving people to just peer in awe over the allotment fence. The experimental allotments drew interest from nurserymen who regularly offered him large sums of money for the rights to propagate the lupins. These offers were all refused; he did not consider the plants ready to go out into the world.

Eventually, in 1935, James 'Jimmy' Baker of Baker's Nursery of Codsall, near Wolverhampton, came to see Russell with a proposal to take over the propagation and promotion of his lupins. The offer also included a house close to where the lupins would be grown. With no mention of money at any point, a deal was struck with the proviso that Russell, now in his seventies, retained control of the overall selection of the plants which would now be known as 'Russell lupins'. A total of 1,500 plants were taken from York to Boningale, Baker's new thirty-acre site where Russell's new house awaited him.

At the 1937 Chelsea Flower Show, over twenty-five years after he began his selecting, George Russell's lupins were finally introduced to the public and unsurprisingly won a gold medal. That year 80,000 people flocked to Boningale nursery to view the marvellous multicoloured lupins in situ. A selection of plants were offered to the public for the first time the following year. They were so successful that Russell lupin seeds became a valuable commodity and were kept in sacks in a bank vault. Russell had finally achieved and released his ideal flower into the world for everyone to enjoy.

George died in 1951, aged ninety-four, and was buried in Boningale, near Codsall, in an unmarked grave at his request. In the year he died, he was awarded the MBE for services to horticulture. *The Times* obituary said of him, he 'banished forever the old-fashioned blue lupin'.

Victoria 'Vita' Sackville-West
(1892–1962)

Victoria Mary Sackville-West is better known to modern
audiences by her nickname 'Vita'. A poet and author of
some repute, she is known, along with husband Harold
Nicolson, for creating the gardens at Sissinghurst Castle,
Kent, purchased in 1930. Harold established a framework
for Vita's instinctive planting, resulting in abundant
flowerbeds in the now iconic series of garden 'rooms', each
with a different theme or colour. In order to finance the
garden work, Vita wrote a weekly gardening column for the
Observer newspaper between 1946 and 1961. These were
later compiled into the most enjoyable and informative
books, *In Your Garden*, *In Your Garden Again* and *More
For Your Garden*. Despite her love of gardening, in
response to a query about the imminent demise of certain
plants, she declared, 'I am afraid my answer is that I don't
know and I don't much care.'

THE PRESIDENT'S MAN

Oregon grape

Mahonia aquifolium syn. *Berberis aquifolium*

Mahonia aquifolium was named in honour of the Irish émigré Bernard McMahon or M'Mahon (1775-1816) who had fled Ireland to America in a bid to escape the political turmoil in his home country. When finally settled in Philadelphia, he quickly established a nursery and botanic garden, named Upsal Botanic Garden, which would indicate that he had previously experienced an element of horticultural and botanical training. Little did he know that he would become a close ally of an American president, as well as being instrumental in an expedition that would lead to the widespread cultivation of *Mahonia aquifolium*.

In 1803, Thomas Jefferson (1743-1826), the third US president, tasked his personal secretary Meriwether Lewis (1774-1809) and explorer William Clark (1770-1838) on a government-sponsored expedition, to explore America's western regions, with a particular focus on the Pacific Northwest – territory that was still 'unclaimed' by colonial standards. The expedition was said to have been planned at McMahon's house.

As the expedition progressed, Lewis and Clark collected hundreds of specimens and other natural curiosities, which they sent back to Jefferson in Washington, DC. The plants and seeds were entrusted to McMahon, who served as curator for the new collection of plants (technically the property of the government). They had to be raised at McMahon's nursery under secrecy in quarantine-like conditions. Lewis had first noticed *M. aquifolium* in the vicinity of the Cascades of Columbia, between the Washington and Oregon states. Its distinctive yellow flowers are followed by black-purple berries similar to bunches of grapes, hence the common name Oregon grape.

McMahon was the first person to cultivate the plant in a domestic setting. The plant already had a long history of its ethnobotanic properties, the Indigenous Peoples used it for a wide range of medicinal applications – the roots and inner bark produce a vibrant yellow dye and when shredded it could be used for basketwork. McMahon was said to be so excited with the range of plants growing from the new seeds that he kept writing to Jefferson, giving him a running commentary.

The expedition's herbarium specimens were handed over for classification to Frederick Pursh (1774–1820), a German botanist who was living in McMahon's house. Initially, Pursh considered naming *M. aquifolium, Lewisia ilicifolia*, then changed his mind before assigning it to the existing *Berberis* genus. Therefore, it became *Berberis aquifolium*, appearing as such in Pursh's 1813 publication *Flora Americae Septentrionalis* or *Plants of North America*.

The popularity of *Mahonia aquifolium* reached new heights at the Princes Nursery, also known as the Linnean Botanic Garden at Flushing, New York. The plant was still sold as the 'Holly leaved barberry or *Berberis aquifolium*', with a hefty price tag of $25. William Prince bemoaned the fact that: 'Several persons have killed this plant by superfluous attention, and by treating it as a tender shrub.'

Incidentally, in 1823, young Scottish botanist David Douglas visited the region and noted in his journal, 'At 8 o'clock this morning we set off for Flushing and visited the establishment of Mr Prince. I found him a man of but moderate liberality, he has some good specimens of Magnolia, of *Berberis Aquifolium*.' Douglas also visited McMahon's nursery, but did not find him at home. Among the haul that Douglas sent back to the Horticultural Society in London was *M. aquifolium*. When it reached Britain in the 1820s, as with any novel specimen, it was very expensive to buy, costing £10 per plant. However, by 1837 the price had plummeted to a still expensive five shillings (£15), as demand for it rose and its supply increased.

McMahon was one of the first nurserymen to advocate the horticultural and ornamental value of native flora and encouraged the readers of his numerous publications to look close to home for worthy plants. In 1818, two years after McMahon's death, Thomas Nuttall, who had been a frequent guest at McMahon's nursery, created the genus *Mahonia*. In his genera of *North American Plants*, Nuttall acknowledged that the new genus was 'in memory of the late Mr Bernard McMahon, for his ardent attachment to botany, and successful introduction of useful and ornamental horticulture into the United States'.

In 1899, *M. aquifolium* was declared the state flower of Oregon, and the plant remains one of the 226 pressed and dried original specimens in the Lewis and Clark Herbarium, now housed at the Academy of Natural Sciences of Drexel University in Philadelphia.

McMahon was often described as Jefferson's gardening mentor and when he published his popular book *The American Gardener's Calendar* in 1806, it was described as Jefferson's horticultural bible. Much of McMahon's advice and planting ideas can be seen in practice at the gardens of Monticello, Jefferson's personal plantation. Not bad for an adventurous young Irishman whose name will forever be connected with the golden yellow flowers and multi-seasonal interests of *Mahonia aquifolium*.

David Douglas
(1799–1834)

In 1823, the Scottish plant collector David Douglas travelled to the Pacific coast of North America on three separate trips on behalf of the Horticultural Society of London. Douglas subsequently introduced over 240 species of plants into Britain and was the first person to collect seeds from many large coniferous trees, which later transformed a multitude of parks, gardens and estates. Notable among them was the Douglas fir, *Pseudotsuga menziesii*, in 1827. It honours a rival Scottish botanist, Archibald Menzies, who had explored the area thirty years earlier. Douglas' specimens enriched Victorians' borders and fuelled the trend for 'pineta', a collection of pine trees or other conifers, which became popular in large estates. He died in mysterious circumstances in Hawaii. His tombstone bears the epitaph: 'an untiring traveller, … died a victim of science'.

HOME COMFORTS

Brompton stock

Matthiola incana 'Brompton stock'

Like many heavily scented blooms, stocks were very popular in the sixteenth- and seventeenth-century garden. At the height of their popularity, Gerard appears to have been quite scandalised about the medicinal properties of *Matthiola incana*, but would not elucidate further. In his *Herball*, he cryptically wrote that it was only used 'amongst certain empirics and quacksalvers, about love and lust matters, which for modesty I omit'. This reticence, from someone usually so forthcoming with his opinion, is somewhat intriguing.

One particularly beautiful crimson double stock was identified before 1714 at the Brompton Park Nursery, London. By 1724, with additional colours, it became known as the Brompton stock Gilliflower.

These delightful flowers later cast a spell upon the rather curmudgeonly travelling companion of the horticultural writer Henry Phillips (1779-1840). In 1824, Phillips described a journey to Normandy in the summer of 1814. Among this party was a gentleman who could find nothing in France to please him. He complained about everything – from the thin soup, the bitter coffee, the unintelligible language to the roads which were far too straight! He thought the women were unattractive and their petticoats were too short, and the peas – yes, peas – were too sweet. Finally, having listened to their companion grumbling incessantly, the passengers were relieved to find a rustic old inn that further irritated the prickly gentleman.

Ready to start sharing any perceived inadequacies of the inn, the gentleman glanced out of a window into a small garden where several very fine stocks were growing. Smiling, he declared that it was the first good thing he had seen since leaving Sussex. On enquiring whether they were Brompton stocks, the hostess confirmed that they were indeed '*Giroflier de Brompton*', and he promptly insisted on treating the whole party to '*un déjeuner à la fourchette*', a 'fork lunch' or buffet. On their departure, the now mollified gentleman left with a Brompton Stock flower in his buttonhole, and a spring in his step. Now and then for the rest of the journey, he exclaimed, 'Thanks to the Brompton stock.' Perhaps he knew whatever Gerard would not share with us.

NATURE'S TIME PIECE

Four o'clock plant

Mirabilis jalapa

Mirabilis jalapa, with its striking diversity of colours, was cultivated in Central and South America long before the arrival of the Spanish in 1519. Even today *M. jalapa* can be found among the ruins of ancient civilisations across the regions. It is grown for its medicinal properties, as well as for its ornamental and highly fragrant flowers, which last only a night and are replaced the next day. The French call it '*Belle de nuit*', beauty of the night. Like most plants pollinated by nocturnal pollinators attracted by the scent, as darkness falls the orange blossom fragrance intensifies.

The seeds of *M. jalapa* were brought back to Europe by the Spanish in 1540 and by the time Gerard wrote his *Herball* in 1597, he had been growing the plant for some years. It has fleshy tuberous roots which Gerard 'lifted' like dahlias and overwintered inside in a 'butter firkin' or small wooden cask filled with sand. Gerard praised the plant's 'brave mixture' of colour, which could be an assortment of red, white, pink or yellow and, in some cases, a striped or mottled combination all on the same plant. *Mirabilis* means marvellous and is a shortened form of *admirabilis*, which the plant certainly is. By some botanical marvel (and for reasons still unknown), *M. jalapa* routinely opens its flowers around four o'clock, hence one of its common names, the four o'clock plant.

In his 1751 publication, *Philosophia Botanica*, Linnaeus had observed over a number of years how certain plants, including *M. jalapa*, consistently opened and closed their flowers at particular times of the day. He concluded that, if it was possible to arrange different plants in the sequence of their flowering 'time', a person could establish a type of floral clock, or '*horologium florae*'.

Interestingly, in its native habitat *M. jalapa* was said to be so habitual in its opening, the plant was grown in prominent places and used to determine the time of day.

A GENTLEMAN'S WAGER

Chatham Island forget-me-not

Myosotidium hortensia syn. *Myosotidium nobile*

E ndemic to the Chatham Islands, off the east coast of New Zealand, *Myosotidium hortensia* is the sole member of this genus. A specimen collected from a garden on the islands in 1838 by Captain Jean Baptiste Cécille was first described in 1846 by the Belgian botanist and director at the Jardin du Plantes in Paris, Joseph Decaisne (1807–82). Yes, he of the ominous looking dead man's fingers tree, *Decaisnea fargessii*.

By 1849, the plant had caught the attention of excited gardeners when it was exhibited at the Horticultural Society of London by Mr Watson, a florist from St Albans, Hertfordshire. It was pronounced to have large 'deeply furrowed glossy dark green foliage', with 'the most beautiful Forget-me-Not-like pale blue flowers each edged with white'.

As magnificent as *M. hortensia* was, it turned out to be a little fastidious in its cultural needs and a challenge to grow and maintain. Several methods of cultivation were put forward with varying degrees of success, including a mulch of rotten fish, seaweed and shark's carcasses, presumably on account of its native habitat just above the high tide mark. This need to succeed where others were failing attracted the attention of wealthy Victorian landed gentry with the time and money to indulge the plants' fussy requirements. In places such as the west coast of Scotland, Ireland and Cornwall, land owners began to create exotic, sheltered coastal gardens full of plants arriving from parts of the world with a similar damp, maritime climate. Head gardeners were encouraged by their employers to pamper these giant forget-me-nots to produce bigger and shinier leaves.

The fashion for woodland gardens at the time suited *M. hortensia*, where its impressive evergreen foliage could be admired all year round. Each year bets were placed among the owners as to who would produce the largest plants with the biggest leaves. A well-grown specimen of *Myosotidium hortensia* is a splendid thing, but as I have discovered, it is an all-or-nothing plant that has firmly refused to grow for me in landlocked Shropshire.

THAT WINDSWEPT LOOK

Cyclamen-flowered daffodil

Narcissus cyclamineus

A 'blonde bombshell on the back of a motorbike'. That is how, as an aide-mémoire, I was first introduced to *Narcissus cyclamineus* by my wonderful lecturer in horticulture during our dreaded obligatory plant identification sessions many years ago. This intense golden yellow miniature daffodil is a native of Portugal and southern Spain. It is very distinctive because of its slim trumpet and swept back petals that are reminiscent of a *Cyclamen* flower, hence its name. For such a quirky little plant, it has a remarkable history.

The story of the handsome young man Narcissus in Greek mythology is a familiar one. Having caught a glimpse of his beautiful face mirrored in the still waters of a pool, he fell in love with his own reflection. Spellbound and unable to tear himself away from his own beauty, he pined away, leaving only a flower, the *Narcissus*. This is where the word 'narcissist' is derived from and, in the language of flowers, the *Narcissus* is associated with egotism and vanity.

One of the first records of *N. cyclamineus* was in 1608 when the artist Pierre Vallet published his *Le Jardin du roy très chrestien Henry IV, Roy de France et de Navare* (a second edition was published in 1623, rededicated to the new king, Louis XIII). Later, the Renaissance French flower painter Daniel Rabel (1578-1637) grew *N. cyclamineus* and other species of *Narcissus,* which he illustrated and described in his magnificent 1622 florilegium, *Theatrum florae.* Seven years later, John Parkinson, in his *Paradisi* of 1629, also depicted the same unusual little flower and described another ninety-three types of narcissi being cultivated in Britain at that time. The majority of these species from Rabel and Parkinson's gardens became entirely lost to cultivation for hundreds of years.

In 1837, the Honourable Rev. William Herbert (1778-1847), also known as Dean Herbert, came across one of the seventeenth-century illustrations of *N. cyclamineus*. As a leading authority on the hybridisation of bulbous plants, including narcissi, Herbert scornfully dismissed it out of hand as 'an absurdity that would never be found to exist'. How wrong can a person be?

Then along came 'the Daffodil King', Peter Barr (1826-1909), who had developed a passion for narcissi and vowed to collect every known species of daffodil in Britain and Europe. He diligently poured over all the old herbals and other sixteenth- and seventeenth-century publications, in particular Parkinson's tome, and listed the ones that were no longer in cultivation, determined to reintroduce them to gardens. In his pursuit, Barr communicated with people all over the country and abroad, including the Anglo-Portuguese botanist Alfred Wilby Tait (1847–1917) who lived in Oporto. Tait became a regular correspondent and aided Barr in his quest to find some of Parkinson's 'lost' daffodils.

In 1886, Tait sent Barr a few bulbs of *N. cyclamineus*, and when they flowered the following February, they won a First-Class Certificate at the Royal Horticultural Society (RHS) show. In the same month, Barr set off on his travels; his first stop was at Tait's in Oporto.

While searching for daffodils, Barr constantly referred to Parkinson's engravings for accurate identification of any specimens he came across. In early May, as Barr travelled further afield, he arrived at Vigo, Spain, close to the Portuguese border, where he found lodgings with a family. After showing them an illustration of *N. cyclamineus*, they directed him to an area not far from their house where he found a colony growing in abundance, and he took vast quantities of bulbs to sell in his London nursery.

After five months of plant-collecting, he returned home briefly before returning seven months later. Now thoroughly smitten with the newly rediscovered *N. cyclamineus*, he collected nearly 3,000 more bulbs, which he later advertised in his nursery catalogue as a 'novelty flower re-introduced into cultivation after a lapse of 200 to 300 years'.

At the time, daffodils were considered unfashionable. However, spurred on by the new and increasing interest and because bulbs are so easy to transport while dormant, Barr exploited the growing region of various species. By the 1890s, he was importing thousands of wild-collected specimens, which he reintroduced and also hybridised. It is unclear just how many of Parkinson's 'lost' narcissi Barr actually managed to track down, but it does raise the question: what would Dean Herbert have said had he lived to see a living specimen of *N. cyclamineus*, which is now quite rare, in the wild?

John Parkinson

(1567–1650)

A royal apothecary and botanist (working under both James I and Charles I), John Parkinson was one of the first to appreciate the cultivation of garden plants for their ornamental rather than their perceived medicinal or other practical properties. His 1629 *Paradisi in Sole Paradisus Terrestris* (which may be translated as 'Park-in-sun's earthly paradise', a pun on the author's name) is a key work in plant history, representing illustrations and descriptions of almost 1,000 plants found in a pleasure garden – as opposed to those found in kitchen or herb gardens. Parkinson had a garden at Long Acre, near London's Covent Garden, which was 'well stocked with rarities' and his writings were based on his own experience of gardening. His second work, *Theatrum botanicum* (or the 'Theatre of plants', 1640), described some 3,800 plants, both indigenous and introduced, which he divided into seventeen categories including one of 'venomous sleepy and hurtful plants'. Its subtitle, *An Herball of Large Extent*, referenced the fact Parkinson believed his volume contained all the plants from 'all parts of the world.'

A DOMESTIC HUNTER

Catmint

Nepeta 'Six Hills Giant'

The English botanist John Ray (1627-1705), referring to the common catmint *Nepeta cataria*, said, 'If you set it, cats will get it. If you sow it, cats won't know it.' Ray was alluding to the fact that when newly planted, handling bruises the plant, releasing its volatile oils, which are irresistible to cats who inevitably destroy it. If seeds are sown, however, our feline friends prove none the wiser.

We owe the introduction of the outstanding *Nepeta* 'Six Hills Giant' to British horticulturalist, collector and nurseryman Clarence Elliott (1881-1969). Elliott travelled extensively on plant-hunting expeditions, his one stipulation being that any plants he collected 'should be good in the garden'. When he wasn't trawling the world in search of plants, Elliott managed his Six Hills Nursery in Stevenage, Hertfordshire. At weekends, he visited old and sometimes forgotten gardens and nurseries throughout the country, looking for potential garden plants. It was during one of these local plant hunting trips that he spotted a clump of *Nepeta mussinii* in a small garden, but one plant had larger flowers and stood head and shoulders above the others. He managed to get some offshoots, which he duly propagated and introduced to the public in 1935. As a result, *Nepeta* 'Six Hills Giant' is a hybrid of unknown garden origin. It has become indispensable in flower borders up and down the country, especially when planted en masse.

The 'Six Hills Giant' is derived from the six Romano British burial mounds that lie beside a Roman road, now the Great North Road, south of Stevenage, and are situated close to the site of the nursery. The Six Hills (or barrows) form the largest surviving Roman barrow group in England and are classed as a Scheduled Ancient Monument. Elliott's nursery closed in 1954 and today the six barrows stand on an island of green amid a built-up area.

Although not as ferociously attractive to cats as the common catmint, one particular little black cat regularly flings itself shamelessly at the clumps of *Nepeta* 'Six Hills Giant' in my own garden.

BY THE LIGHT OF THE MOON

Jasmine tobacco

Nicotiana alata syn. *Nicotiana affinis*

I n her 1916 publication, *My Garden*, the American garden designer and writer Louise Beebe Wilder (1878-1938) had nothing but praise for *Nicotiana alata*. 'The perfume of the White Tobacco is very delicious at night and the tubular blossoms have a shimmering quality which makes them very charming in the moonlit garden.'

The concept of the white, or moonlight garden is not new, the aim being to extend the enjoyment of a garden into the evening by using plants that are enhanced by reflecting the light of the moon. These flowers also have a fragrance that intensifies in the evenings in their bid to attract nighttime pollinators. One of the earliest moonlight gardens is the Mehtab Bagh situated opposite the Taj Mahal in India. Created in the 1630s, it was commissioned to be a perfect place from which to view the palace. Undoubtedly, *N. alata* would have secured pride of place in this delightful garden.

The genus *Nicotiana* was named in honour of the French ambassador to Portugal, Jean Nicot (1530-1600) who has been associated with the introduction into Europe of *Nicotiana tabacum* in 1560. Nicot also acquired the dubious privilege of being commemorated in the substance nicotine. But for ornamental tobacco, the gardening world had to wait another 270 years for the delightful *N. alata* to emerge.

N. alata was first described in Johann Heinrich Friedrich Link and Christoph Friedrich Otto's publication *Icones plantarum rariorum horti regii botanici Berolinensis* (*Illustrations of Rare Plants in the Berlin Botanic Garden*), in 1830. These plants had been grown from seeds sent by German botanist and naturalist Friedrich Sellow (1789-1831) from southern Brazil to the botanic gardens in 1827. *N. alata* reached Britain in 1829, possibly from France. Meanwhile, the plant had migrated northwards from Brazil, through Latin America into the United States of America in the early 1800s.

Its luminous flowers and intoxicating evening scent made it the perfect plant for inclusion in the extensive and extraordinary moonlight or white garden, created at Indian Hill Farm, West Newbury, Massachusetts. The garden was begun in 1833 by Benjamin and Mary Perley Poore after travelling to England, perhaps influenced by some of the English flower

gardens they had seen. Their son, the American correspondent Ben: Perley Poore (1820–87) – and yes, the colon was part of his name – subsequently took over the estate and continued the planting of the gardens. The moonlight garden eventually consisted of double herbaceous borders of around 700 feet long and 12 feet wide, stocked with an array of white flowering plants. In order to continue the white theme, Poore added a herd of snow-white cows and oxen, and flocks of white sheep to the view on the hillside above the flower beds, with white pigeons circling in the air around numerous white dovecotes. Even the farm's poultry on the ground was white. It must have been utterly enchanting in the sunshine, as well as when bathed by a silvery moon.

In the mid-twentieth century, the influential Vita Sackville-West created the now iconic White Garden at Sissinghurst, her home in Kent. She wrote, 'I am trying to make a grey, green and white garden. This is an experiment which I ardently hope may be successful, though I doubt it ... I cannot help hoping that the great ghostly barn owl will sweep silently across a pale garden, next summer, in the twilight.'

Today the garden continues to shine brightly, with plantings of the abundant, trumpet-shaped white flowers of *N. alata* alongside such dazzling plants as white *Lavatera*, jasmine, antirrhinums, cosmos and a showstopping central arbour smothered in the highly scented, rambling white *Rosa mulligani*. The White Garden albeit composed of greys, silvers, greens and whites, was completed in 1949, just as Vita had envisaged it. It is said to be the most imitated garden style in the world.

Nicotiana alata is another plant favoured by the Victorians that does very well as a plant to bring indoors. You will be amply rewarded by its superb perfume each evening.

A NEW LEASE OF LIFE

Love-in-a-mist

Nigella damascena 'Miss Jekyll'

P ainter, garden designer, gilder, author, carpenter and silversmith, these are just a few of the skills Miss Gertrude Jekyll (1843–1932) possessed in abundance. However, not many people are aware that she was also a prolific plant collector and accomplished breeder, who ran a successful plant nursery for thirty-five years, selling excess plants from her garden. Jekyll, with her artist's eye, used *Nigella damascena* in her clients' gardens as a 'filler plant'. At its absolute finest when planted in generous drifts, its very distinctive flowers, borne above feathery fennel-like foliage, created a pleasantly hazy effect. This possibly gives rise to its more common name of love-in-a-mist. In fact, the similarity in foliage indicates why in the seventeenth century Parkinson and others called it the 'fennel flower'.

Miss Jekyll was an ardent traveller who drew inspiration from the countries she visited, and during these adventures acquired plants which were to become characteristic features in her designs and recurring subjects in her literature. Not only did Jekyll introduce plants from her travels but she actively rescued and promoted plants at home that were perceived as being 'old fashioned' and in danger of disappearing from gardens and nurseries altogether. On discovering a once celebrated plant languishing in a weed-filled corner, she reclaimed it, nurtured it and gave it a new lease of life before sharing it with her friends or offering it for sale to her many customers. A born entrepreneur and astute businesswoman, she not only sold plants but also ran a cut flower business which she operated from a window on the north side of the house.

Jekyll kept immaculate documentation of all the plants she sold between 1903 and 1929. This included plants such as *N. damascena,* a plant said to have been brought back from Damascus to Britain around 1570.

Like many plants of such longevity, nigella's popularity has waxed and waned over the years, especially in the gardens of people who found themselves frequently carried on the waves of floral fashion. By 1760, an article in the *London Gardener* suggested that *Nigella* had become so common that 'no one should be without for the sake of its strange appearance', but it was deemed unworthy of a place in a small garden.

Nonetheless, *Nigella* remained a firm favourite and an iconic cottage garden flower. Jekyll admitted that she had 'learnt much from these little gardens' and wrote how 'one can hardly go into the smallest cottage garden without learning or observing something new ... two plants growing beautifully together by some happy chance'.

Jekyll's knowledge of plants was vast and for over thirty years she was ably assisted by her Swiss-German gardener, Albert Zumbach, who apparently served her with 'intelligent obedience untainted by ideas at variance with her own'. Albert obviously knew his place! From the 1870s Jekyll acquired, grew, selected and improved her plants of choice, which were then propagated and raised in large quantities in her 'reserve' garden between the house and kitchen garden at Munstead Wood, her home in Surrey. This is where the pale, soft, blue-flowered *N. damascena* 'Miss Jekyll' was bred in the late 1800s. Jekyll was obviously extremely fond of this particular plant, as it appears as the frontispiece to her 1916 publication *Annuals and Biennials*, in which she wrote how 'the variety "Miss Jekyll" was the result of many years' careful selection, and may be said to be the best garden *Nigella*'.

The genus *Nigella* is derived from *niger*, meaning 'black', alluding to the colour of the seeds, which are very small and are produced in their hundreds. They are housed in attractive papery, balloon-like pods, which themselves can be used in dried flower arrangements. The seeds have been used for a variety of household remedies and recipes. One of the most intriguing was recorded in 1561 and involved first burning the seeds and mixing their ashes with bacon fat, which was then combed through the hair in order to rid yourself of lice and 'nittes'. On the other hand, unrequited love and longing also found meaning in the unusual flower - giving someone a bouquet of *N. damascena* meant 'you puzzle me' but it could also indicate doubt, uncertainty and even embarrassment.

Whatever its meaning, *N. damascena* 'Miss Jekyll' was awarded the Royal Horticultural Society Award of Garden Merit in 1895, and still deserves a spot in any garden no matter what the size.

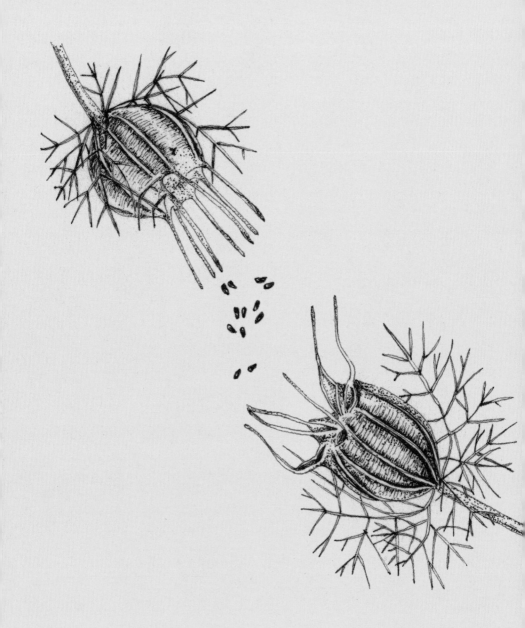

CHALICES OF WHITENESS

Rock's peony

Paeonia suffruticosa 'Rock's Variety'

When the British plant collector Reginald Farrer (1880–1920) arrived in Gansu Province, China in 1913, he was astonished by the sight of a glorious tree peony growing on a hillside. Farrer marvelled at how it made 'one's heart go thump anew each time one sights its wide-frilled chalices of whiteness'. *Paeonia suffruticosa* 'Rock's Variety' is beyond gorgeous; it is flamboyancy personified, with scented flowers. As such, it is hardly surprising that it's a much sought-after plant.

It's alleged that Farrer collected a specimen of the plant, but we cannot be certain. Instead, the rather eccentric Viennese-born American Joseph Rock (1884–1962) introduced it into America, seven years after Farrer's death. Rock, an extremely talented man, was able to turn his hand to anything, and between 1924 and 1927 it was plant-collecting in north-western China under the auspices of Boston's Arnold Arboretum.

Unable to endure the hardships associated with collecting plants in remote places, Rock travelled well. His baggage was stocked with personal belongings aimed at making his journey as comfortable as possible. This included everything essential for a civilised dinner, from damask tablecloths to elegant glassware, a canvas folding bathtub and tailored suits and shirts (you never know who you might meet after all).

In the spring of 1925, Rock travelled to the same region as Farrer had and arrived at a Buddhist monastery at Choni (now Jone), where he saw a white tree peony growing in the courtyard. Realising he was likely looking at the plant fitting Farrer's description, he sent seeds back to the Arnold Arboretum. The plants flowered in 1938, to immediate acclaim and were named *P. suffruticosa* 'Rock's variety' before being distributed to botanical institutions in America and Europe. However, its path was never quite straightforward.

In recent years botanists have spent a great deal of time and effort trying to establish the true status of this beautiful cultivar. It is entirely possible that it is identical to the wild, white-flowered tree peony seen by Farrer. But is it? The mystery surrounding the plant's origins only adds to its appeal as the Holy Grail of peonies for us all.

AN INTERLOPER IN THE BORDERS

Oriental poppy

Papaver orientale

J oseph Pitton de Tournefort (1656–1708), professor of botany at the Jardin du Roi, collected seeds of what we call the oriental poppy while travelling in the Levant in 1700. On seeing the oversized scarlet-orange flowers of the plant, Tournefort recorded: 'We observed ... a very fine species of poppy, which the Turks and Armenians ... do not extract Opium from.' The seeds were sent to Paris and from there to Holland.

By 1714, the poppy was being grown in Britain where it remained in its natural state throughout the Georgian, Regency and Victorian eras for a further 200 years, quietly returning each year, maintaining its popularity in gardens large and small.

In 1903, Amos Perry (1871–1953), a celebrated Edwardian plant breeder and nurseryman, spotted a salmon-pink seedling among the bright red-orange blooms. Perry nurtured and multiplied this plant before putting it on the market three years later as *Papaver orientale* 'Mrs Perry', after his wife, Nancy. Seeing the potential of developing other colours, Perry set his heart on breeding a white one. He crossed and recrossed the palest seedlings to no avail.

Then, out of the blue, he received a letter from a customer complaining bitterly that their perfectly designed pink and red border had been ruined: a 'nasty fat white one had appeared' among them. Unconvinced by this news, Perry did not react until the customer wrote to him once again demanding to know what was to be done. Intrigued, Perry travelled to the garden to see the alleged interloper, which he hadn't been able to grow for himself. Great self-restraint must have been required not to jump for joy in the presence of the disgruntled customer when he saw it was true.

Perry calmly offered to take the offending specimen away in exchange for a handful of *Montbretia* corms. What an absolute bargain – because in 1912 *P. orientale* 'Perry's White' came on the market. Today, the plant's large, pure white flowers, with contrasting purplish spots and stamens in the centre, are welcomed annually with open arms in countless gardens, an eyecatcher holding centre stage, irrespective of any preconceived colour schemes.

A NATIVE'S RETURN

Annual phlox

Phlox drummondii

In 1835, while exploring the southern lands of North America, Scottish botanist Thomas Drummond (1793-1835) sent back what would turn out to be his last parcel home. In fact, Drummond would never see his homeland again. Part of his final consignment were the seeds of a Texan wildflower which would prove to be Drummond's legacy. By 1837, this flower that was to become known as *Phlox drummondii* would have even the most hardened plantsmen swooning over it.

Back in 1831, under the patronage of William Jackson Hooker, later first director of the Royal Botanic Gardens, Kew, Drummond made his second journey to North America. By 1833, he was in Texas, which at the time was still part of Mexico and Drummond became one of the first plant collectors to explore the region. Having dispatched the seeds of *Phlox drummondii* with other findings in February 1835, despite suffering acute ill health, Drummond set off to Cuba.

Hooker, who had been receiving Drummond's keenly anticipated specimens, instead, received three boxes in June 1835 containing only Drummond's meagre personal possessions. These were followed by a letter dated March 1835 from the American consul in Havana, enclosing Drummond's death certificate. The details of these events remain a mystery.

Hooker named the plants grown from the seeds received *Phlox drummondii* in order to, 'serve as a frequent memento of it's unfortunate discoverer'. The plant took the horticultural world by storm and four years after the seeds arrived in Britain, it was declared the 'pride and ornament of our gardens'.

Perversely, in the spring of 1836 the Buel and Wilson nursery in New York acquired seeds from London and distributed them among a selection of nurserymen. *P. drummondii* was presented at the Massachusetts Horticultural Society, eliciting 'universal admiration'. All the seeds were now coming in from London and by the 1870s Americans eagerly sought it out for their gardens, unaware that these new European imports were descended from one of their own native wildflowers, which had returned home as an exotic border and bedding plant.

THE ACT OF A ROGUE OR A FOOL

King protea

Protea cynaroides

In 1881, Sir Joseph Hooker considered the protea to be 'the handsomest of plants, whether for size, form or colour of inflorescence, would carry the first prize at any horticultural show'. Each to their own, I must admit I find proteas rather fascinating but also somewhat sinister and other-worldly. *Protea cynaroides*, South Africa's national flower, with its silvery mass of stamens surrounded by the pink bracts standing stiffly like a crown, and has the largest and most conspicuous flowers of the proteas.

In 1735, Linnaeus chose to name the plant after the Greek sea god Proteus, who could assume many different forms to escape anyone attempting to compel him to predict the future. According to mythology, Proteus knew 'things' but had an aversion to divulging them unless he was held very tightly, which forced him to resume his usual appearance before telling the truth. The fact that proteas have been around for millions of years would indicate that they have, indeed, witnessed a great many things. It is also not surprising that the floriography of the protea pertains to transformation, change and courage.

When naming plants, often taking into account the plant's qualities, Linnaeus derived his generic names from poetry, mythology, the monarchy and promoters of botany and other sciences. He did not always get this right but in the case of the protea he was spot on. The genus *Protea* has over 1,500 species, in different shapes and sizes, from compact plants and shrubs to tall trees. Proteas are indeed a diverse genus and very long lived. The majority of the species are found in the Fynbos, South Africa, an area that demands its plants to be resilient and adaptable to its almost hostile environment.

The largest collection of proteas ever in Britain belonged to Alderman George Hibbert (1757-1837), a very wealthy West India merchant, founder member of the West India Docks. Hibbert's collection, with a total of thirty-five species by 1805, was such that it was even considered to be far superior to the Royal Botanic Gardens, Kew. The majority of Hibbert's proteas had been collected by the Scottish plant collector James Niven (1774-1827), whose plant hunting expeditions he had sponsored. Hibbert's proteas were never made available to the general public for sale, not even to the members of the aristocracy who begged for plants. He would only gift or swap them with his close acquaintance, Empress Josephine at Malmaison, France, and George III.

In charge of this enviable collection was Hibbert's head gardener Joseph Knight (1778–1855), who became one of the first people in the country to successfully propagate and induce proteas to flower; this brought him great accolades from the botanical world. When George Hibbert retired, he gave his living collections, including his proteas, to Knight who had set up a nursery in the early 1800s, selling exotic plants on the King's Road in London's Chelsea. Knight became the first person to commercially cultivate and sell proteas. However, there was big trouble brewing around the corner for him.

It came in the form of an almost reputation-destroying error of judgement. In 1809, Knight published an horticultural essay, 'On the Cultivation of the plants belonging to the natural order Proteaceae'. Bizarrely, his own work amounted to a mere fourteen pages of this essay. A further one hundred pages were contributed by the botanist Richard Salisbury. Unfortunately for Knight, the content of these pages turned out to be fully plagiarised from the botanist and naturalist Robert Brown, a fact not warmly received by the close-knit botanical society. Salisbury was persona non grata and Knight was seemingly tarred with the same brush. It's strange how Salisbury risked his professional and personal reputation for such little reward.

The wronged Robert Brown simply commented of Salisbury: 'I scarcely know what to think of him except that he stands between a rogue and a fool.' Knight kept his head down, continuing to run his thriving nursery while sponsoring his own plant-collecting expeditions. Knight's nursery also became a training ground for budding gardeners.

The hype around proteas began to decline with many specimens dying off, leading to the virtual disappearance of the plant in private gardens. *P. cynaroides* did eventually come back into cultivation after gardeners developed a better understanding of its exacting cultural needs. They have a long vase life in flower arrangements, and make for excellent dried flowers. However, they have never really reached the same heights of popularity as they had in Hibbert and Knight's time.

Carl Linnaeus or Carl von Linné
(1707–78)

Linnaeus was a Swedish naturalist and taxonomist who acquired the moniker *Princeps botanicorum* or Prince of Botanists. Linnaeus's first published work was *Systema naturae* in 1735. He acquired hundreds of plant specimens from a range of people travelling around the world, including his own ex-students, known as his 'Apostles'. Linnaeus is best known for his system of classification, which gave plants a binomial or two-part Latin name, the genus and species. This system was widely accepted by 1768 following the publication of *Species Plantarum* in 1753. This has been recognised as the starting point of modern botanical nomenclature. After being knighted in 1757, he took the name Carl von Linné. His motto was: *'Deus creavit, Linnaeus disposuit'* – 'God created, Linnaeus organised'. The Linnean Society, London, was founded in 1788 by Sir James Edward Smith, who had bought Linnaeus's collections and library from his widow.

AN EARLY INFLUENCER

Mignonette

Reseda odorata

'N ot tonight Josephine,' is a phrase said to have been uttered by
Napoleon Bonaparte one evening while trying to avoid his wife's
amorous advances. Empress Josephine Bonaparte (1763-1814)
has often been portrayed as a flighty socialite, famed for her lavish
entertainments and salacious exploits. So, it may come as a surprise
to many that Josephine, born in the French West Indies, was a very
accomplished plantswoman, gardener and keen botanist who played a key
role in the collection and introduction of many new plants into France and
on to the rest of Europe via her garden at Malmaison. I suppose you could
say that she was an early influencer.

There were not many positive outcomes during Napoleon
Bonaparte's infamous 1798 Egyptian invasion (yes, the same campaign
where Antoine Coquebert de Montbret met his very untimely end; see
Crocosmia × crocosmiiflora, pages 52-55). But one outcome was the revival
of the exquisitely scented *Reseda odorata*, which grows naturally in Egypt.

The seeds of *Reseda* were collected by the young botanist Alire
Raffeneau Delile (1778-1850), who was tasked with creating a botanical
garden while Bonaparte's men were in Cairo. Delile observed that the
Egyptian people called the sweet-smelling plant 'love grass' and the Ancient
Egyptians had used it during funeral rites and ceremonies by placing it in
their tombs. It was also used extensively by the Romans, according to the
Roman statesman and scholar Pliny the Elder (AD 23-79), *Reseda* had the
'power of charming away many disorders'.

R. odorata reached the shores of Britain in 1739, when it was introduced
by Philip Miller (1691-1771), head gardener and curator at the Chelsea Physic
Garden in London, who received seeds from Adriaan van Royen (1704-79),
botanist and professor at Leiden University. Miller described the flower
in 1752 as 'of a dull colour, but having a high ambrosial scent'. By 1787,
the *Botanical Magazine* was suggesting ways in which to best enjoy the
sweet-smelling plant, 'as it is most readily cultivated in pots, its fragrance
may be conveyed to the parlour of the recluse, or to the chamber of the
valetudinarian' - or hypochondriac to you and me.

Napoleon sent Josephine the seeds of *R. odorata*, which she cultivated at Malmaison, before introducing it to her fashionable circle in Paris. The flowers caught the imagination of the French aristocracy and was soon given the name, *mignonette*, or 'little darling'. No garden or drawing room in Paris was without it. The plant's perfume was at its most intoxicating in the morning and early evening and soon became the frontline defence against the less than wholesome odours of the city.

English high society was not far behind in embracing it. City balconies and window boxes were laden with mignonette, rooms adorned with potfuls of the plant when a household was entertaining. As mignonette swept through the parlours of Georgian England, the demand for indoor plants grew.

Manufacturers such as Josiah Wedgewood took full advantage and began to produce special decorative containers to use as mignonette planters and pans. The beau monde, or the fashionable society of Georgian London, regularly hired plants, and mignonettes in beautiful pots were the most sought-after plants from 1811.

Despite the fact that Britain and France were in the grip of the Napoleonic Wars during this period, the Empress Josephine had the most extraordinary influence when it came to plants for her beloved gardens. Over the years, she had managed to establish regular correspondence with a large international network of nurserymen, botanists, plant collectors and gardeners all over the world, including the Royal Botanic Garden, Kew, to the point where British naval officers received orders from the Admiralty with instructions that any captured vessels carrying plants or packages of seeds addressed to the Empress Josephine were to be forwarded without delay.

Many of the flowers associated with Josephine influenced horticultural fashions: a great example was her 250-strong rose collection, which inspired French hybridisers to create beautiful new roses. In the case of *R. odorata*, she set the fashion in Paris for growing it as a pot plant, which then spread throughout Europe to appear in all stylish parlours. Yet, for a plant with such a beautiful fragrance, its actual appearance is rather disappointing; thus, the contrast between the dullness of its flowers and its far superior perfume meant that if you received a bunch of mignonette, it was not a good omen, the message being 'your charms exceed your beauty'!

Mignonette is just one of the ways in which the Empress Josephine helped to advance the ideas and practices of botanical exploration and plant exchange globally. Unlike her somewhat egomaniacal husband, she crossed all political, religious and social boundaries to play a pivotal role in expanding botanical knowledge on an international level.

OUT OF SIGHT, OUT OF MIND

Common rhododendron

Rhododendron ponticum

This particular plant tends to ruffle a few feathers. *Rhododendron ponticum* in full flower is lovely – I once had an evening frock in that same luscious lilac shade that made me feel like a million dollars! It is, however, extremely invasive – estate managers and head gardeners up and down the country are at their wits' end trying to eradicate or control it within their gardens and woodlands, which are being stifled under canopies of the shameless *R. ponticum*.

When it was first introduced into the country in 1763, *R. ponticum*, a native of Gibraltar and the Levant, was treated as a tender exotic, to be mollycoddled at every turn. It was recorded by Swedish botanist Clas Alströmer (1736–94), in an area close to a Carmelite Convent between Cádiz and Gibraltar around 1750. Plants were later imported from there to Britain.

R. ponticum proved to be an absolute joy for those with very deep pockets. Yes, believe it or not there was a time when *R. ponticum* was advertised by nurseries with no price, thus, confirming that old adage, if you have to ask the price of something, you obviously cannot afford it.

The plant's bright clusters of flowers and dark green glossy foliage quickly found favour in that quintessential feature of the late Georgian garden, the shrubbery. By the 1800s, each spring large quantities of forced plants were brought to the London flower markets, which saw an increase in the number of plants brought into the house for seasonal decoration.

This included compact specimens of *R. ponticum* forced into flowering earlier in the season, and then transferred into decorative blue and white Delftware planters or cachepots before serving as indoor plants. 'Cachepots', from the French *cacher*, 'to hide', were used to conceal the plain clay growing pot for indoor display. So, how did this beautiful plant become such a botanical pariah?

When not being pampered for the parlour, thousands upon thousands of *R. ponticum* were sold throughout the country, with many being planted across all the large estates. Wealthy Victorian landowners soon discovered that the plant self-seeded freely, which they encouraged, initially. In 1841, Philip Frost (1804–87) the head gardener at Dropmore Park,

Buckinghamshire, proudly wrote to *The Gardener's Chronicle* concerning the thousands of self-sown *R. ponticum* seedlings on the estate: 'it is very easy to fill woods ... a man and a boy can collect enough seeds to sow acres in a few hours'. Perhaps the alarm bells should have been sounding then.

Aided by the growing popularity of the country house weekend party, *R. ponticum* proved to be an ideal cover for game, in particular pheasants. Shooting as a weekend pastime was on the increase and swathes of these plants were planted across the wider landscape. Newly introduced and less pushy types of rhododendrons, in an array of stunning colours, from various parts of the world, were routinely grafted on to thousands of *R. ponticum* rootstocks. The burgeoning trend for more naturalistic and woodland planting championed by William Robinson, ensured that beautiful, riotously coloured rhododendron dells were planted across many estates, parks and private gardens. Very soon, Mother Nature, encouraged by the human hand, inadvertently collaborated in the hybridisation of a tougher and hardier race of plants which relished the British climate. The genie was well and truly out of the bottle.

Colonies of rhododendrons tended to be planted some distance from the house and main garden, and so technically were out of sight and at most times, out of mind. Yet *R. ponticum* threw out suckers that eventually overwhelmed the enfeebled exotic scions. Vibrant-coloured and rare specimens gradually reverted back to the original charming mauve of the *R. ponticum* and began to self-seed, unwittingly providing the perfect storm, which would later see it as a botanical and conservational nightmare.

R. ponticum is now covered by the Wildlife and Countryside Act 1981, which states that it is illegal to plant it in the wild or to allow it to encroach into other areas from your property. Still, for a short period of time each year, the sight of this delightful menace flowering en masse is a most uplifting sight.

A HEART OF GOLD

Matilija poppy

Romneya coulteri

Linnaeus' introduction of the binomial system enabled plant collectors, botanists and gardeners to speak the same European language, Latin, when identifying a plant. But what of the plant's indigenous name and associated myths that would have formed part of the people's lives who coexisted with that species for hundreds of years before? Along the coast of California, the Chumash peoples valued the Matilija poppy for its medicinal properties in treating skin conditions and in easing the digestive system.

Said to get its name from Chief Matilija, the flower is part of Chumash mythology. According to legend, the chief's daughter, Amatil, was in love with a handsome warrior who was tragically killed in battle. Inconsolable, she laid herself upon her lover and there she died. On that very spot a beautiful flower grew, with pure white silken petals, symbolising their love, and a bright yellow centre, representing Amatil's heart of gold.

Centuries later, in 1832, along came the Irish Botanist and physician Thomas Coulter (1793-1843), a man with a passion for lizards and snakes, which he carried about with him in his pockets while he explored California. Among the specimens he recorded were the seeds of the Matilija poppy.

Coulter returned to Ireland in 1834 with a vast herbarium, which he began to arrange and classify, but he died before he could complete this monumental task. It was Professor William Harvey at Trinity College Dublin who introduced many of Coulter's Californian plants into cultivation. The Matilija poppy gained a new identity when Harvey named it *Romneya coulteri* after a close friend of Coulter, the Reverand Thomas Romney Robinson, any reference to the Chumash culture gone.

In 1876, when the plant was displayed in public, it was reported that 'one spectator just stared at the flower for a full hour'; it's so easy to see why. The flower has been wonderfully likened to 'a great butterfly drying its wings after it leaves the chrysalis.'

A RELUCTANT GARDENER UPROOTED

John Ystumllyn's rose

Rosa 'John Ystumllyn'

Each year, with great fanfare, new roses are launched by prestigious rose breeders from around the world at various flower shows. These roses, which tend to commemorate well-known people in the public eye or members of their family, are the culmination of years of investment in time, money, great expertise and a labour of love. According to the plant historian Alice Coates (1905-78), when choosing a rose, look for one that has been named after the grower's wife. If she is of a grumpy disposition, she will refuse to have her name associated with a bad rose; equally if she is of an affectionate nature, she will be honoured with a fine flower. Of course, this also applies to women naming roses after their spouses.

One recently launched yellow rose has made history. *Rosa* 'John Ystumllyn' honours Britain's first well-recorded Black person and horticulturalist in North Wales. The initiation for the development of the rose was inspired by Zehra Zaidi who grew up in South Wales. A lawyer, humanitarian and founder of We Too Built Britain, she has long campaigned to raise awareness of the achievements of people from under-represented groups and of ethnic minorities to see themselves represented in the wider community and in everyday life.

In 1746, roughly aged eight, a small boy playing by a stream in a woodland, according to his own account, was abducted by slave traders, from an unknown location in West Africa, a region which was the cornerstone of the transatlantic slave trade. The exact route of his arrival into Britain is unclear but the boy eventually ended up in the ownership of the Wynne family of Plas Ystumllyn, near Criccieth, North Wales, who gave him the name John Ystumllyn. We will never know what his real name was.

Here he was taught to speak and write in English and Welsh and trained in horticulture, an occupation in which he excelled, especially in the cultivation of flowers as a gardener on the estate. It was also recorded that he was a skilled carpenter. Unusually for that time, in May 1754, when John was about sixteen, a portrait was commissioned from an unidentified artist, in which he is depicted, dressed in a neckcloth, waistcoat and jacket.

Ystumllyn became known locally as 'Jac Du' or 'Jack Black' and, in 1768, at Dolgellau, he married Margaret Gruffydd, a local housemaid from the Wynn estate. John later became a land steward not far from Criccieth and after a short period working away, he and Margaret returned to work for the Wynn family. In recognition of their services to the family, they were given a cottage with a large garden. The couple had seven children, five of whom survived, and several of their descendants still live in the area today. Ystumllyn died in 1786. His sandstone memorial at St Cynhaearn's Church, Ynyscynhaearn, Gwynedd is now Grade II-listed.

In a bid to raise Ystumllyn's profile, and as a celebration of his life, Zaidi approached the Hertfordshire-based rose breeders Harkness Roses with the idea of creating a rose to commemorate him. Harkness did not disappoint. The resultant hybrid tea rose Rosa 'John Ystumllyn' is a beautiful buttery yellow with a most pleasant scent – historically, yellow roses have been symbols of friendship and companionship, so this seemed an apt way to celebrate the man.

The rose was officially named in 2021 and launched at 2022's RHS Chelsea Flower Show. It was later planted in the gardens of Buckingham Palace in the weeks leading up to the Queen's Platinum Jubilee celebrations. Queen Elizabeth II (1926–2022) stated: 'The rose has been bred as a mark of friendship and community, and I hope guests and visitors to the garden will have the opportunity to reflect on what this rose represents for many years to come.' Twenty roses were also planted around Criccieth Library near where Ystumllyn lived.

Like the proverbial London buses, you wait ages for one, and then two come along at once. Only a year later at the 2023 Chelsea Flower Show, a second rose breeder, David Austin Roses launched a rose named after Dannahue 'Danny' Clarke (1960–), the British horticulturalist and garden designer, known as 'The Black Gardener' who rose to fame in the BBC's *Instant Gardener*. *Rosa* 'Dannahue', an English shrub rose, is a light peachy-apricot colour with a fruity fragrance.

Ystumllyn's portrait is at Plas Dinas, Gwynedd, and there is an engraving of it at the National Library of Wales. I believe both *R.* 'John Ystumllyn' and *R.* 'Dannahue' symbolise a move towards the recognition of under-represented people in gardening, horticulture and other land-based vocations.

A BUFFALO'S FURY

Bird of paradise

Strelitzia reginae

Plant collecting has always been a dangerous occupation. Scottish botanist Francis Masson (1741-1805), 'the king's collector', has long been associated with the introduction to Britain of *Strelitzia reginae* via Sir Joseph Banks. There is no account of Masson's first sight of this exquisite plant, however, there is a dramatic first-hand description of how Swedish botanist Carl Peter Thunberg came across *S. reginae* in his *Travels in Europe, Africa and Asia between the Years 1780-1799.*

Thunberg was accompanied by his guide, Johan Auge, superintendent of the Dutch East India Company's Cape Town garden, and a soldier named Leonardi. On 3 November 1772, the little party was ambushed by a very cross buffalo who took exception to the trespassers. The furious animal killed a horse and badly injured another before stomping off to pick a fight elsewhere.

In the ensuing mayhem, Thunberg, sensible man that he was, had scrabbled up the nearest tree from where he could observe the chaos unfolding until the buffalo retreated. After scrambling down, he looked for his fellow travellers. He described the sight that greeted him: 'Sitting fast like two cats on the trunk of a tree with their guns on their backs ... and unable to utter a single word ... the sergeant at length burst into tears, deploring the loss of his two spirited steeds; but the gardener was so strongly affected, that he could scarcely speak for some days after.'

In the days following this emotional encounter, Thunberg struck out on his own, only to come across *S. reginae* in full bloom. He wrote how 'the strelitsia [sic], with its yellow flowers and blue nectarium, grew near this spot, and was one of the most beautiful plants, of which the bulbs were procured to send to Europe'. Obviously, he meant rhizomes, which he sent to the Leiden and Amsterdam Botanic Gardens in early 1773. Thunberg later heard from the locals of a rogue buffalo which was so spiteful that it had been driven out by its herd and was obliged to live alone. If only he had known.

FORCED TO PERFECTION

Common lilac

Syringa vulgaris

The scent of flowers has always been a highly valued characteristic when choosing a bouquet for any occasion at whatever time of year. So, when a plant comes along with flowers that look as luscious as it smells, it is bound to become a much sought-after commodity. In particular, white, scented lilacs have long been representative of purity and innocence, although this cannot be said of the French naturalist and alleged spy Pierre Belon (1517-64), the first person to record *Syringa vulgaris*, the common lilac, in 1554.

Belon published his findings about the plant in *Observations of many oddities and memorable things ...*, following his illicit travels around several eastern Mediterranean countries. He described how the Turkish people loved flowers and, in particular the lilac, which was 'almost an elbow long, of a violet colour, ... as big as a Regnard's tail' (a fox's tail). As he travelled, Belon took an intense interest in the secrets surrounding the medicinal properties of certain plants that France wanted access to. He always carried a copy of Avicenna's *Canon of Medicine* (c. 1012), which gave the Arabic names for combinations of plant extracts. Despite frequenting the tiny specialist shops known as 'druggists', the response from the proprietors was hostile, as it would be to any over-inquisitive enquirer. Unsurprisingly, on his return to Paris, Belon was assassinated in the Bois de Boulogne, it was said by his close friends: he simply knew too much.

In 1562, the Flemish diplomat and herbalist Augier Ghislain de Busbecq (1522-92) returned home to Vienna with not only a specimen of Belon's 'fox's tail' but also an illustration. The Italian botanist Pietro Andrea Mattioli (1501-77) used Busbecq's drawing in 1565 to produce the first woodcut image of the plant that he called lilac. When Busbecq moved to France in 1570, he took some of his beloved lilac with him, and was credited with introducing it to Paris, where it soon began to fill the city's gardens, thereby laying down the foundation of the local florists' dream of a year-round lucrative product.

The seasonality of certain flowers has allowed us to mark the unfolding year, but the cut flower industry has always found ways to outwit Mother

Nature by forcing plants into flower, out of season. The art of forcing lilac blooms commercially, especially for the white version, had been practised in France as early as 1774 in caves and cellars. Because, remarkably, no matter the natural shade of the flower, when non-white lilacs are forced in the dark, they produce white flowers. The darker the flower, the whiter the result and so the 'white lilac' industry was born. One particularly deep dark purple sort, first grown at the Château de Marly gardens, near Versailles, in 1808, became known as *lilas de Marly* and proved to be very popular for forcing.

Enormous, specially heated forcing sheds were located in and around the southern suburbs of Paris in order to cater to the overwhelming demand for the fragrant white lilac flowers. Lilacs form their flower buds in late summer before becoming dormant. Therefore, the forcing process started in the summer months, when gardeners working in the lilac groves pulled up long shoots or rods of the plant with at least five years' growth. The shoots with a small root ball were bundled up and kept dormant inside the sheds, until winter. These were then planted in multiple rows very close together in rich soil within the forcing sheds. The doors and windows were sealed to exclude all light, and any glass was covered with *paillassons*, or straw mats, before the heating process began. An even temperature of 40 degrees was maintained and within three weeks the buds would open – however, most were stripped by hand to leave just the uppermost to flower into perfection. The perfume must have been overpoweringly intoxicating in these sheds, especially when the flower stems were harvested late in the evening. The flowers were then boxed and kept cool before being packed onto trains and steamers destined for the flower markets of London, Paris and other European cities, and even as far as St Petersburg in Russia.

The almost miraculous appearance of these heady pure white blossoms was a great source of curiosity. The Victorians adored the delicious aroma of lilacs, but were equally scandalised by what they called its 'boudoir scent'.

Although the forced lilac industry continues to supply florists worldwide, thanks to the dedication of hybridisers such as Victor Lemoine (1823-1911) and his wife, Marie Louise (1834-1905), we can now grow white lilacs of our own, such as the double white, highly fragrant *Syringa vulgaris* 'Madame Lemoine', bred originally in 1894.

Lilacs can easily live for more than a hundred years and veteran specimens are often found in old, neglected and abandoned gardens, delightful survivors of an age when they were the absolute height of fashion and not in the least bit 'common'.

GUIDING SOULS

African marigold

Tagetes erecta

In 1683, the British agriculturalist John Worlidge (1640–1700) described the African marigold as 'a Fair bigge yellow flower, but of a very Naughty Smell.' *The Floricultural Cabinet,* and *Florists Magazine,* in 1849, implied that the flower's large bright flowerheads were an attempt to distract from its unusual odour akin to 'those persons who depend more on their wardrobe than their conduct for making themselves agreeable'. Is this unfair? Certainly, the African marigold has a 'look at me' attitude – as for its distinctive musky smell, this comes mostly from the stem and foliage when crushed or bruised. It's proved useful to deter pests from crops, its strong scent keeping them at bay.

A native of Mexico and South America, the flower derives its common name from the route by which it appeared to enter Europe. The Aztecs, in Mexico, had bred and valued marigolds for thousands of years, not only for their ornamental or medicinal properties but also for their integral part in the cultural rituals of honouring the dead. The *De la Cruz-Badiano Aztec herbal* (also known as the *Libellus de medicinalibus Indorum herbis*) of 1552 recorded the marigold's magical powers, which enabled a person to 'cross a river or water safely'.

This idea of a safe passage is echoed in the annual Mexican ceremonies in celebrating the annual *Día de los muertos* or Day of the Dead on 2 November. The dead are considered to still be members of the community and, on that day, they temporarily return to earth. The marigold, known as *flor de muertos,* or 'the flower of the dead', plays a key role because of its bright colour and strong scent, the petals strewn from the gravesite to altars in houses to guide returning souls of deceased loved ones back home. Clusters of the flower also decorate the altars where the deceased's favourite possessions and food are laid out.

Thousands upon thousands of *Tagetes erecta* are used to decorate graves, and as a result marigolds grow prolifically in cemeteries. In 2008, UNESCO declared the Day of the Dead an Intangible Cultural Heritage of Humanity, which reflects and highlights the growing awareness of many important worldwide cultural practices.

BREAKING A FEVER

Rembrandt tulip

Tulipa 'Absalon'

T he most fascinating thing about the tulip is that it has never possessed any medicinal properties nor served a utilitarian purpose (granted, when prepared safely the bulbs were eaten as a last resort during times of extreme food shortages). It has little or no scent, so essentially tulips have never had any real purpose to justify their enormous presence in our gardens, apart from sitting there and just looking gorgeous. At nearly 250 years old, *Tulipa* 'Absalon' is a beautiful relic of a time when people valued this flower above all else.

For hundreds of years, travellers and collectors have taken plants from distant lands and brought them back in their wild forms to be hybridised and cultivated into new garden varieties. But when tulips emerged out of Turkey in the sixteenth century, if not earlier, they were already a thing of beauty and sophistication, with diverse colours and forms, having been in cultivation there for centuries.

Various people were instrumental in their introduction from Turkey via Austria into the rest of Europe. The person who popularised them, from 1570, was the French botanist and physician Carolus Clusius (1526-1609). He sent the first bulbs to England around 1578, as noted by the English traveller and geographer Richard Hakluyt who remarked in his 1582 publication, *The Principal Navigations, Voyages and Discoveries of the English Nation,* that: 'within these foure yeeres there have bene brought into England from Vienna ... divers kinds of flowers called Tulipas, ... procured thither ... by an excellent man called M. Carolus Clusius'.

Back on the continent, the flower's popularity grew quickly as its novelty caused a rise in demand, and prices increased. Shrewd, quick-thinking merchants, as well as some tulip growers began to make a lot of money. To add a frisson of delight, some of the mainly single colour tulips started to display coloured stripes, streaks or swirls of contrasting colours over the yellow or white background. Holland, in particularly was hit the hardest in its desire for these almost magical flowers. Between 1634 and 1637, the most coveted flowers became these rare and mysteriously 'broken' tulips.

Enormous sums of money changed hands as bulbs, real or speculative, offered the potential to make anyone's fortune. This game of chance culminated in the well-recorded frenzy 'tulipomania' or *tulpenwoede*, literally 'tulip fury'. But unbeknown to these frantic buyers, once the bulb's flower had broken, it grew weaker until it stopped flowering altogether.

These 'breaking' symptoms had been first recorded in 1576 by Clusius. '[A]ny tulip thus changing its colour is usually ruined afterwards ... only to delight its master's eyes with this variety of colours before dying as if to bid him farewell'. This is why the most famous and very expensive tulips like 'Semper Augustus' (red-and-white stripes) in the 1630s, and 'Viceroy' (white, streaked with purple) in 1637, gradually became extinct. The reason behind the flowers' strange behaviour, which led to Clusius' prophetic words, were not discovered for another 352 years.

When the tulipomania bubble finally burst, 'never again' the people cried. True to their word, when the stirrings of hyacinth mania began to emerge nearly a hundred years later, in the 1730s, the Dutch government swiftly printed a warning in 1734 to head off a potential new flower 'fury'.

In the intervening years the inexplicable tulip 'breaking' had taken on mythical proportions that confounded breeders for centuries. In 1780, *Tulipa* 'Absalon' became one of these beautiful aberrations, characterised by the swirling pattern of a rich burgundy-brown over a yellow background.

So, what sorcery was this that had led to the previous tulip madness? The answer was finally revealed in 1927 by Dorothy Mary Cayley (1874–1955), a mycologist working at the John Innes Institute (now the John Innes Centre). She discovered that the 'breaks' which produced these beautiful tulips, so prized during tulipomania, were actually caused by a virus spread by aphids. By grafting one half of an infected bulb to a healthy half, the virus could be transmitted. Why did the answer not come sooner, people ask? The word 'virus' wasn't understood in the modern sense until the 1880s, and the electron microscope, which enabled researchers to track the virus, was not developed until the 1920s.

Since that time, infected or naturally broken tulips have come and gone; in fact, they were usually promptly destroyed for fear of infecting any surrounding plants. But this cursed beauty also enables us to preserve tulips like 'Absalon', whose colouration appears to be the result of a natural occurrence and so has not succumbed like other broken tulips.

T. 'Absalon' is a stable and long-flowering variety, a true antique garden flower but one that serves to remind us of a time when the tulip became more beautiful and desirable as the result of a disease that could only lead to their ultimate extinction.

THE JOY OF THE GROUND

Lesser periwinkle

Vinca minor sp.

M arion Dudley Cran (c.1875–1942) was one of those wonderfully talented women whose legacy seems to have faded into obscurity. In August 1923, almost a year after the British Broadcasting Company (BBC) was founded, Cran began a radio programme focusing on gardens and gardening. She was not only the first gardening radio broadcaster but the first woman to achieve this honour. Cran had a particular love of periwinkles and is responsible for the reintroduction of an old variety.

Cran came to prominence in 1913, following her bestselling book *The Garden of Ignorance,* which was aimed at people attempting to establish gardens of their own. Cran's ability to transport her listeners, who were mainly women, to beautiful gardens and introduce them to new plants for their gardens, ensured her resounding success on the 'wireless', and, when enquiring letters came in regularly, she was encouraged to write further books.

In 1928, she wrote *The Joy of the Ground,* which recounted the events in her own garden at her fourteenth-century home, Coggers, in Benenden, Kent. One day, while walking down a lane not far from her house, her fondness for periwinkles drew Cran's attention to one growing under a hedge. She wrote: 'it was a reddish wine colour ... I had never heard of such a flower before'. This was indeed a rare find.

The more familiar pale blue or blue-violet flowered periwinkle, with its habit of wandering freely, had been cultivated for over thousands of years, becoming naturalised in Britain and throughout much of Europe. Similar to snowdrop colonies, the common periwinkles are often indicators of former human habitation.

The poet Edward Thomas (1878–1917) put it so well at the beginning of his poem, 'The Tale', when he wrote:

There once the walls
Of the ruined cottage stood,
The periwinkle crawls,
With flowers in its hair into the wood.

The common name of periwinkle is a corruption of the Latin *pervincula*, meaning 'ties', a reference to the plant's long, strong and supple stems, which were used for tying or binding things together.

On discovering this unusual red periwinkle near her home, Cran swiftly transplanted a clump into her garden where it began to flourish. She gave a cutting to a close friend who, after consulting her copy of John Parkinson's *Paradisi*, realised that he had known of this particular plant in 1629. He wrote: 'the most ordinary sort is of a pale blew colour, ... and some of a darke reddish purple colour'. Since Cran's house was over 600 years old, she came to the conclusion that 'her red periwinkle' was an escapee from the garden centuries ago. The joy of the ground was the common name used for the lesser periwinkle from the fourteenth century.

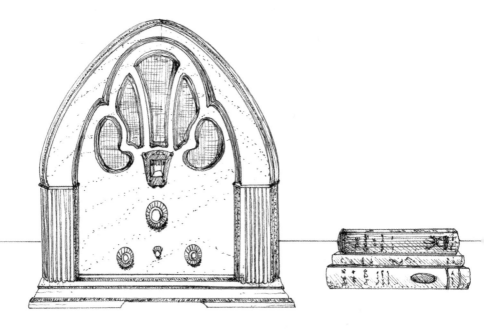

In her final radio broadcast in 1931, before a return visit to South Africa where she was born, Cran shared the story of the little red periwinkle and offered some to any listener who could give it the best home. She received hundreds of letters. She duly divided the plant into as many little slips as she could and waved them off. Cran's only stipulation was that as these plants were free gifts, those who received it should keep it so: they could be gifted, from gardener to gardener but never sold, thus ensuring that the 'joy of the ground' would be truly shared.

When she returned to Coggers, Cran's periwinkle was still thriving, and judging by the amount of correspondence she received from recipients of her *vinca*, it appeared to be flourishing in gardens across Canada, America and South Africa. Over the years, Cran calculated that over 6,000 little plants had been shared globally.

Marion Cran regularly encountered her red periwinkle. One afternoon while travelling about and visiting gardens, she came across an elderly man tending his pretty little cottage garden in a small village. Cran spotted a periwinkle and asked if it was the red sort, which, indeed, it was. It transpired that his daughter had given it to him because he was fond of the reddish colour. He proudly told Cran, 'she had it off the wireless'.

Sadly, like Marion Cran herself, her little red periwinkle which bound her to so many radio listeners and gardeners across the world now appears to have retreated back into the shadows. Doubtless 'the joy of the ground' will be growing, unidentified, in some corner of a garden waiting to be rediscovered by another eagle-eyed plant lover.

Perhaps it seems only fitting that, in the language of flowers, the *vinca* is given to symbolise the pleasures of memory.

SCENT BY RAIL

Sweet violet

Viola odorata

Viola odorata is an adorable but most peculiar little plant. In 1629, John Parkinson, eagle-eyed as ever, noticed that it set seed without the flower opening – meaning self-pollination occurred inside a closed flower. It therefore has cleistogamous flowers. It's a bit like changing into a swimming costume under a towel, possibly why *Viola odorata* later became a symbol of modesty.

Sweet violets had been grown commercially for centuries, but the introduction of several new species from Eastern Europe in the early nineteenth century contributed to violet growers producing exciting new varieties that were hardier, had larger flowers and longer stems – so much better for cutting.

One Sunday in 1871, George Lee (1817–1913), a fruit and violet grower, returned from church and went to his nursery at Tickenham near Clevedon, Somerset. Still feeling spiritually uplifted, Lee knelt to pray, and on opening his eyes spotted an outstanding violet seedling growing among his strawberries. He named it *V. odorata* 'Victoria Regina' in honour of Queen Victoria.

The French violet growers had been supplying the British markets, but the sad little bundles were often past their best by the time they arrived. Being closer to home, Lee's new cultivar was received with great enthusiasm and admiration and soon bunches of *V. odorata* 'Victoria Regina' were being packed and transported all over the country, arriving still fresh courtesy of the Great Western Railway from Clevedon station.

Due to its popularity, *V. odorata* 'Victoria Regina' became known as the 'Clevedon violet' and was described as having 'surpassed all the other violets at London's Covent Garden flower market'. By 1883, demand led the papers to report that the railway station at Clevedon had the distinction of 'perfume creeping out of the railway parcel offices, to the astonishment of strangers'.

Today, sweet violets can still be found growing among the old hedgerows in and around Tickenham – small clusters of a bygone era when a prayer was answered, an industry flourished and the scent of violets lingered through railway carriages and waiting rooms.

WHAT'S IN A NAME?

American wisteria

Wisteria frutescens syn. *Glycine frutescens*

Throughout the world the two most widely cultivated species of wisteria are *Wisteria sinensis*, from China, and the Japanese *Wisteria floribunda*, but not many people know of their North American cousin, *Wisteria frutescens*.
This summer flowering species was the first to be introduced into Europe in the early eighteenth century. Its seeds were collected in May 1722 by the English naturalist Mark Catesby (1682-1749), during his second visit to South Carolina. Catesby sent seeds of what he described as the 'Carolina kidney bean tree' to various interested parties back in England, including the horticulturalist Robert Furber (1674-1756) at his Kensington nursery, in London, where it flowered for the first time in this country. In 1727, Furber published a catalogue that included the plant, simply labelled as 'Mr Catesby's new climber'.

Furber, a respected member of the Society of Gardeners, excelled in the importation and propagation of plants from America and he commissioned the Flemish artist Pieter Casteels III (1684-1749) to design a series of broadsheets featuring seasonal plants in bloom. They became known as the *Twelve Months of Flowers* and were later engraved and hand coloured. In 1731, the American wisteria was featured in the July edition, taking pride of place in among a bouquet of other mid-summer flowering plants. A year later, these monthly catalogues were reissued in a smaller format under the title *The Flower Garden Display*, and this time it was called the 'Carolina kidney bean'. Furber wrote 'this plant makes a very good shew, bringing long spikes of purplish blossoms'.

Once established, the plant was highly sought after and exclusively cultivated for over sixty years by some of the most notable botanists and gardeners of the eighteenth century. By 1789, it was being grown at the Royal Botanic Gardens, Kew as *Glycine frutescens*, the name ascribed to it by Linnaeus in 1753. *Glycine*, the name still used in France, comes from the Greek *glykys* meaning 'sweet'.

In 1818, the Anglo-American botanist Thomas Nuttall (see page 189) observed differences in the flowers of the genus *Glycine*, which included the soy bean *Glycine max*, so he created the new genus *Wisteria*. The name honoured the anatomist Professor Caspar Wistar (1761–1818) who had just died. Wistar's family was of German heritage and their original name had been Wüster. When they immigrated to America, they, like so many others before and after them, anglicised their names in order to help their assimilation into society, but one branch of the family chose Wistar and the other Wister.

In the second volume of his book, *The Genera of North American Plants*, published in 1818, Nuttall described *Wisteria*, with an 'e': adding a footnote confirming that the name was to commemorate the late Professor Caspar Wistar who in his opinion was 'a philanthropist of simple manners, and modest pretensions, but an active promoter of science'. This spelling of *Wisteria* was repeated in the index: it was not, as some thought, a clumsy mistake. Nuttall was very good friends with Charles John Wister (1782–1865) a keen naturalist and a cousin of Professor Wistar. Wister was a member of the Linnaean Society of Philadelphia and frequently went on botanical excursions with Nuttall.

In some literature, the genus *Wisteria* is often still spelt '*Wistaria*', however, and this is invariably shrugged off as a misprint. For many years, botanists have wondered how such an intelligent and well-educated man as Nuttall could have made such a glaring error when honouring someone whom he greatly admired. So, what happened?

It has been recorded that Nuttall had confided to Charles that the name *Wisteria* had a better ring to it than *Wistaria*. Therefore, one can only conclude that Nuttall chose the generic *Wisteria* to indirectly honour both sides of the renamed Würsters. It's the thought that counts after all ... Since that time the American wisteria has been overtaken in popularity by its showier and more rampant Chinese and Japanese cousins. However, all is not lost, as there are now several *Wisteria frutescens* varieties available, with the added advantage of being more compact. All in all, they have proved more than capable of standing their ground.

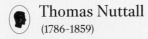

Thomas Nuttall
(1786-1859)

Nuttall was an Anglo-American naturalist who travelled from Liverpool to Philadelphia when he was twenty-two. There, the naturalist Benjamin Smith Barton of the University of Pennsylvania persuaded him to collect and work on the flora of America. Nuttall joined several scientific expeditions between 1811 and 1834, and was one of the first botanists to travel overland to the Pacific coast. He was so focused on collecting plants that his single-mindedness reportedly made him oblivious to personal risk, fuelling his reputation as an eccentric. In his quest to further science, he ruined his rifle by storing seeds in the barrel and frequently used it for digging up plants, effectively rendering the weapon useless. This earned him the nickname *'le fou',* the fool. Nevertheless, Nuttall compiled a comprehensive flora of America before becoming curator of the Harvard University Botanic Garden. The terms of an inheritance in 1841 required nine months of residence in England each year, so he came home, where he became known as the 'father of Western American botany'.

EVERLASTING PARLOUR DOMES

Everlasting strawflower

Xerochrysum bracteatum syn. *Helichrysum bracteatum*

A flower arranger's dream, *Xerochrysum bracteatum*'s crisp and papery bracts appear almost artificial. The Victorians were great admirers of the natural world, the more unusual the better. The extraordinary flowers of *X. bracteatum* were a curiosity, which when displayed under a glass case or parlour dome, was guaranteed to spark animated conversations.

Xerochrysum bracteatum was collected in May 1770 by Joseph Banks and Daniel Solander, who were part of Captain James Cook's first voyage on the HMS *Endeavour*, while in search of the 'unknown southern land'. It is unclear what happened to the original specimen collected. In 1800, an expedition led by Nicolas Baudin landed in Australia, and returned to France with specimens including the seeds of *X. bracteatum*. They flowered at Château de Malmaison in 1803, and were included in Étienne Pierre Ventenat's *Jardin de Malmaison*, a catalogue of the plants growing in the gardens.

From 1860, the fashion for dried, artificial silk, crepe and even wax flowers in parlour domes increased the demand for plants like xerochrysums, which had the dubious distinction of being equally attractive dead or alive. These whimsical parlour domes, often exhibited in pairs, were used to display and preserve anything from nightmarish taxidermy, a grim Victorian fascination, to artfully arranged flowers. In 1880, the British-born American seedsman James Vick (1818–82) declared: 'The Everlastings, or Eternal Flowers, have of late attracted a good deal of attention in all parts of the world. … and make excellent bouquets, wreaths, and every other desirable winter ornaments.'

In contrast to the limited lifespan of fresh flowers, dried xerochrysums retain both their form and colour for many years. The flower's longevity once it has been dried led it to become a symbol of immortality. Some of the more ostentatious parlour dome arrangements became family 'heirlooms' and were bequeathed on to some unlucky distant relative. *Xerochrysum bracteatum* has been accused of 'behaving like a professional beauty who refused to grow old, in their quest of everlasting beauty'. Harsh but probably fair.

FOR WANT OF A POLLINATOR

Spanish dagger, Adam's needle

Yucca gloriosa

The first recorded flowering of a yucca in Britain was in 1604 at Stubbers, North Ockenden, Essex, in the garden of the gentleman botanist William Coys (1560-1627). It caused such a sensation when the tall pyramid of creamy white flowers reached 6 feet that it earned the name *gloriosa*. Stubbers was a well-known destination for botanists and gardeners from home and abroad. The Flemish physician and plantsman Matthias de l'Obel (1538-1616) visited the garden while the yucca was in flower. He was so impressed he created an illustration entitled '*the most gloriously exalted Yuca*'. Away from the garden, he became equally animated about Coys' methods of brewing beers and ales.

This was a great achievement for Coys. Twelve years earlier, *Herball* author John Gerard had received a yucca plant from Thomas Edwards, an apothecary from Exeter. According to John Parkinson, Edwards had obtained it through one of his servants who had recently returned from the West Indies. Gerard's plant had still not flowered by the time he published his *Herball* in 1597. It later died when an attempt was made to move it to another garden after his death in 1612. Parkinson acquired his own yucca plant from the London merchant John De Franqueville, a celebrated 'florist' of rare plants who in turn had obtain it from Vespasien Robin (1579-1662) botanist to the King of France. In a twist to the botanical tale, Vespasien confirmed that the original plant, the first seen in France, had been given to his father Jean Robin (1550-1629) by none other than Gerard himself.

Parkinson studied his plant at great length and observed that because of its rarity, anyone in possession of this plant would be 'loth to cut any thereof, for feare of spoiling and losing the whole roote'. In 1629, he wrote that a type of cloth could be made from the threads in the leaves, but he found them too strong and hard for that particular usage. These ideas were not far off the mark because in its native habitat the Indigenous Peoples traditionally used the yucca's leaf fibres to make sandals, baskets, cords and mats. Its fruits, called 'datile', were edible, and the roots contained saponin, used as soap. But as with many plants introduced into this country from fields afar, the yucca was destined to be valued purely for its ornamental properties.

A far more pressing matter was that of seeds – Parkinson keenly observed that in England and France the yucca's flowers simply fell off after blooming. It took 243 years to understand the reason for this routine lack of seeds. In 1872, while working as the state entomologist of Missouri, United States, the British-born Charles Valentine Riley (1843–95) observed that the yucca plant depended on a family of night-flying moths for its fertilisation. This is why the flowers, as dusk approaches, raise themselves up and expand to exude a powerful scent. The female yucca moth, *Tegeticula yuccasella*, uses the flowering plant exclusively to lay her eggs. The larvae, when they hatch, only feed on some of the seeds, leaving enough of them to develop and mature. Just before the seed pod opens, the pinkish caterpillar drops and burrows into the ground, sealing itself in a cocoon to emerge later as an adult moth. Essentially, the yucca and its pollinator have co-evolved over thousands of years.

Yucca gloriosa is not unique in this mutualistic relationship: the climbing orchid *Vanilla planifolia*, which is indigenous to Mexico, can only be pollinated by the tiny Mexican *Melipona* and *Euglossine* bees. This interdependency between plants and their natural pollinators demonstrates how the relocation of plants to the other side of the world can impact on the fragile balance of nature.

Over the years, the yucca has been cherished and championed by people like the Scottish botanist and garden designer John Claudius Loudon (1783–1843), who suggested that if it were planted in large pots it would make a great substitute for the equally spikey Mediterranean *Agave* in 'imitating Italian scenery round an Italian villa'. Another cheerleader of the yucca was Gertrude Jekyll who frequently used the yucca as a 'dot plant' or exclamation mark to bring architectural texture and dramatic contrast within her garden design schemes.

Gertrude Jekyll
(1843–1932)

Influential Gertrude Jekyll came to gardening relatively late in life, having had to abandon her earlier passions of painting and other complex crafts due to progressive myopia. She channelled her creativity into designing gardens by bringing a painterly eye for colour and plant textures to her designs. She travelled extensively and from 1863 collected plants from the wild in Britain and throughout Europe, taking them home to 'improve' them for her clients. In 1889, she established a partnership with architect Edwin Lutyens (1869–1944). They were the original gardening dream team and collaborated on about one hundred of the 400 gardens that Jekyll created in Britain, America and Europe. She was a great promoter of using traditional arts and crafts to enhance her designs, fostering ideas of the correct relationship of a house, its garden and plants. Jekyll also authored thirteen books and contributed to the leading gardening magazines of the day.

A LATE BLOOMER

Youth and age

Zinnia elegans

T he yellow and rather plain form of *Zinnia peruviana*, a wild species, was possibly the original zinnia in Europe, which anatomist and botanist Johann Gottfried Zinn (1727–59) illustrated and erroneously assigned in 1757 to the *Rudbeckia* genus. In 1759, Linnaeus recognised the similarities between Zinn's plant and a previous specimen, which he had described himself back in 1753, which turned out to be *Z. peruviana*. Realising Zinn's misunderstanding, Linnaeus changed the genus from *Rudbeckia* to *Zinnia* in a posthumous nod to Zinn for his contribution to botany.

In 1792, Dutch scientist Nickolaus Joseph von Jacquin (1727–1817) was sent wild collected seeds from Tixtla de Guerrero, Mexico, by Spanish botanists Martín Sessé and José Mariano Mociño – the resulting plants were *Zinnia elegans*. This was later introduced into Britain in 1796 by Charlotte, Marchioness of Bute (1746–1800) after she acquired seeds from Professor Casimiro Ortega of the Royal Botanic Gardens, Madrid, while her husband was serving there as the British ambassador.

Z. elegans belongs to the group of flowers that had been around for a very long time, just hovering on the edge of stardom, waiting to be noticed and fully appreciated. Throughout the nineteenth century, hybridising and selection were concentrated on more compact forms, with an increasingly wide range of colours. Their contribution to the fashionable Victorian bedding schemes was immense. The garden writer Shirley Hibberd wrote in 1861 how the new '*Zinnia elegans* flore-pleno is a really superb thing' and that it was the season's 'leading agent in the bedding system'.

Over in America, influential plant breeder Luther Burbank (1849–1926) had spent several years developing the most remarkable zinnias. When he died, Stark Brothers of Louisiana acquired the breeding rights to Burbank's plants, adding to their own less illustrious collection of zinnias. Their 1927 seed catalogue showcased a brightly coloured selection of 'Stark Zinnias'. These popular flowers could now be seen in most American gardens.

It was within the Stark brothers' home state that the African American folk artist Clementine Hunter (1887–1988) found immeasurable inspiration in the colourful flowers. She was born at the notorious Hidden Hill cotton plantation in Louisiana, where her grandparents had been slaves and her parents were sharecroppers. The estate was reported to have inspired the author of the controversial 1850s' book *Uncle Tom's Cabin; or, Life Among the Lowly*. Hunter picked cotton in the fields there before she became a domestic servant at neighbouring Melrose Plantation, a liberal and creative retreat for artists. In 1939, at the age of fifty-two, while cleaning a recently vacated guest room, she came across discarded tubes of paints and brushes left by a visiting artist. Hunter, who never learnt to read or write, began to paint. One of her first paintings in that year was on a piece of corrugated cardboard and titled *Bowl of Zinnias*, a favourite subject that she constantly returned to over the years.

As the century progressed and Clementine Hunter embarked on her unexpected painting career, her beloved zinnia was undergoing an intensive breeding programme several states away in Pennsylvania. A heightened interest in the flower resulted in acres of land being devoted to the breeding and selection of the flower. As people experimented, in search of commercially successful combinations, each year dahlia-like, cactus-flowered, chrysanthemum-like and 'quilled' forms of zinnias in striking colours were introduced.

These were the types of zinnias that Clementine Hunter painted and became so fond of. Hunter painted from memory, and although most of her themes were quirky recollections of life on the plantations, she also became a prolific painter of colourful jugs filled with the bright flower heads of zinnias. After working all day, she painted at night, aided by a kerosene lamp. She produced over 5,000 works during the second half of her life. Although illiterate, with practice she was able to 'sign' her paintings with a backward 'C' over an 'H' similar to a Chinese character.

In 1956 Hunter became the first African American to achieve a solo art exhibition at the Delgado Museum, now the New Orleans Museum of Art. However, because it was held in a segregated venue in Louisiana, she was not allowed entry into the building to see her work on display. Her work continued to be held in high regard, and in the 1980s she was invited to the White House to meet Jimmy Carter. She never made it to Washington, DC – her response to the invitation, 'Well President Carter knows where I live, so he can visit me'!

Youth and age, the zinnia's rather obscure common name, is said to be because the young buds appear in abundance, even while the mature flowers are still blooming, refusing to fade for weeks, even after their youth has passed. This could also be said of Clementine Hunter, maintaining her youthfulness through her vibrant compositions. Hunter frequently depicted herself in her garden where she grew the beautiful zinnias that have become inextricably linked with her artistic legacy.

Hunter died aged 101 on New Year's Day 1988. The stage play, *Zinnias: The life of Clementine Hunter* by the playwright Robert Wilson premiered in 2013 and in the same year one of Hunter's zinnia paintings was exhibited in the Louvre, in Paris. The icing on the cake was the State of Louisiana declaring in 2019 that 1 October would become Clementine Hunter Day.

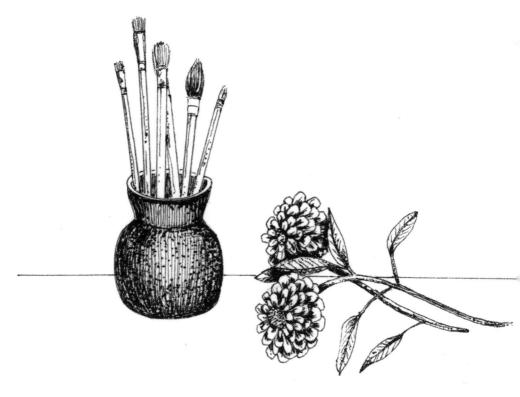

SELECTED BIBLIOGRAPHY

Beidleman, Richard G. 2006. *California's Frontier Naturalists*. California: University of California.

Biggs, Matthew. 2018. *The Secrets of Great Botanists and What They Teach Us About Gardening*. London: Mitchell Beazley.

Bisgrove, Richard. 2008. *William Robinson: The Wild Gardener*. London: Frances Lincoln.

Blunt, Wilfred. 2004. *Linnaeus, The Compleat Naturalist*. London: Frances Lincoln.

Boddy, Kasia. 2020. *Blooming Flowers: A Seasonal History of Plants and People*. New Haven, CT: Yale University Press.

Cambell-Culver, Maggie. 2001. *The Origins Of Plants*. London: Headline.

Coats, Alice M. 1956. *Flowers and Their Histories*. London: Hulton Press.

Drori, Jon. 2021. *Around the World in 80 Plants*. London: Laurence King.

Duthie, Ruth. 1988. *Florists' Flowers and Societies*. London: Shire Publications.

Elliott, Brent. 2001. *Flora: The Illustrated History of the Garden Flower*. Richmond Hill, ON: Firefly Books.

Gardener, Chris, Musgrave, Toby and Musgrave, Will. 1980. *The Plant Hunters: Two Hundred Years of Discovery and Adventure Around the World*. Boston, MA: Cengage Learning.

Gerard, John. 1597. *A Herball, or Generall Historie of Plants*. London: John Norton.

Graustein, J.E. 1967. *Thomas Nuttall, Naturalist*. Cambridge, MA: Harvard University Press.

Grimshaw, John and Ward, Bobby. 1998. *The Gardener's Atlas: The Origins, Discovery, and Cultivation of the World's Most Popular Garden Plants*. Richmond Hill, ON: Firefly Books.

Grissell, Eric. 2020. *A History of Zinnias: Flower for the Ages*. West Lafayette, IN: Purdue University Press.

Hibberd, Shirley. 1871. *Rustic Adornments for Homes of Taste*. Portland, OR: Timber Press.

Himansu Baijnath and Patricia A. McCracken. 2019. *Strelitzias of the World: A Historical and Contemporary Exploration*. London: Jacana.

Jekyll, Gertrude. 1916. *Annuals & Biennials, the Best Annual and Biennial Plants and their uses in the Garden*. London: Scribner.

Kingsbury, Noel. 2016. *Garden Flora: The Natural and Cultural History of the Plants in Your Garden*. Portland, OR: Timber Press.

Knapp, Sandra. 2022. *In the Name of Plants: Remarkable plants and the extraordinary people behind their names*. London: Natural History Museum.

Lawrence, Sandra. 2022. *Miss Willmott's Ghost: The Extraordinary Life and Gardens of a Forgotten Genius.* London: Blink Publishing.

Leese, Brenda. 2023. *There She Grows Again: Wives, Royalty, Goddesses.* Cumbria: Pixel Tweaks Publications.

Mickey, Thomas J. 2021. *All About Flowers: James Vick's Nineteenth-Century Seed Company.* Athens, OH: Swallow Press.

Nisbet, Jack. 2009. *The Collector: David Douglas and the Natural History of the Northwest.* Seattle, WA: Sasquatch Books.

Parkinson, John. 1629. *Paradisi in Sole Paradisus Terrestris.* London: Hvmfrey Lownes and Robert Yovng.

Potter, Jennifer. 2013. *Seven Flowers and How They Shaped Our World.* London: Altantic Books.

Robinson, William. 1899. *The English Flower Garden.* London: John Murray.

Sacheverell, Sitwell. 1939. *Old Fashioned Flowers.* New York: Charles Scribner's Sons.

Sackville-West, Vita. 1951. *In Your Garden.* London: Michael Joseph.

Stearn, F.C. 1956. *Snowdrops and Snowflakes.* London: Royal Horticultural Society.

Stout, A.B. 1934. *Daylilies.* New York: Macmillan.

Stuart, David. 2002. *The Plants that Shaped our Gardens.* London: Frances Lincoln.

Sutton, S B. 1974. *In China's Border Provinces: The Turbulent Career of Joseph Rock.* New York: Hastings House.

Way, Dr Twigs. 2005. *A History of Women in the Garden.* Gloucestershire: The History Press.

Wells, Diana. 1997. *100 Flowers and How They Got Their Names.* North Carolina: Algonquin.

Wilkinson, Anne. 2012. *Shirley Hibberd, the Father of Amateur Gardening: His Life and Works, 1825-1890.* Worcestershire: Cortex Design.

Wulf, Andrea. 2009. *The Brother Gardeners: Botany, Empire and the Birth of an Obsession.* London: Windmill Books.

INDEX

ABOUT THE AUTHOR

Advolly Richmond is a plants and gardens historian, TV and radio presenter and independent researcher in social history. She lectures on garden history subjects from the sixteenth to twentieth centuries and contributes garden history features on *BBC Gardeners' World* and presents plant history profiles for BBC Radio 4's *Gardeners' Question Time*. She is also the presenter of *The Garden History Podcast, an A–Z*. Advolly is passionate about promoting garden history in all its branches and likes to encourage people to value their garden and landscape heritage. She has written numerous articles and features on plants and historic gardens for a variety of publications. She is a plant-loving practical gardener with probably far too many roses and an ever-growing collection of snowdrops.

ABOUT THE ILLUSTRATOR

Sarah Jane Humphrey is an award-winning botanical artist who has won four RHS Medals, including the 2023 Gold medal for her collection of seaweed paintings. Much of her work is published in books and magazines and she has an array of high-profile clients, including the Royal College of Physicians, BrewDog, the Eden Project, the Duchy of Cornwall and Jo Malone.

Photo © Alexandra Green

ACKNOWLEDGEMENTS

I would very much like to thank Quarto Publishing and in particular Alice Graham for commissioning this book in the first place. Having seen the pictures of your beautiful daughter, I have thoroughly forgiven you for disappearing off on maternity leave. I hope that this is the book that you envisioned. To Melissa Smith, who was tasked with looking after me, thank you for your calm and gentle supervision, your unwavering support when the going got very tough, but most of all, I am grateful to you for your compassion and reassurances. My heartfelt thanks also go to the design, editorial, publishing and marketing teams behind the scenes who have helped to deliver this book.

Enormous kudos to the fabulous Sarah Jane Humphrey, whose exquisite botanical illustrations have brought this book to life; I am in awe of your talent. Also to Dianne Barre, my fellow garden historian whose generosity of spirit and positive demeanour has motivated me through many of my endeavours, and to Andrea Belloli, for her expertise that gave me the courage to say yes to writing this book. I would also like to acknowledge the artist and horticultural historian Alice Coats (1905–78) whose publications sparked my interest in plant history.

My daughter, Tilly, who has been a great cheerleader from the start and her infectious enthusiasm knows no bounds. Much love to all my family and friends who have uttered words of comfort and encouragement.

I am especially indebted to my husband, Paul, for his kindness, patience, his enhanced cooking skills and unconditional love; I thank you.

Quarto

First published in 2024 by Frances Lincoln Publishing
an imprint of The Quarto Group.
One Triptych Place, London, SE1 9SH
United Kingdom
T (0)20 7700 6700
www.Quarto.com

A catalogue record for this book is available from
the British Library.

ISBN 978-0-7112-8222-3
EBOOK ISBN 978-0-7112-8223-0

10 9 8 7 6 5 4 3 2 1

Assistant Editor: Kat Menhennet
Commissioning Editor: Alice Graham
Designer: Masumi Briozzo
Project Editor: Melissa Smith
Publisher: Philip Cooper
Senior Production Controller: Rohana Yusof

Printed in China